LOVE NOT THE WORLD
WINNING THE WAR AGAINST WORLDLINESS

RANDY LEEDY

*To Mom & Dad,
with love &
appreciation for
all that the Lord
has used you to do for
me over the years.
May the Lord bless
you!*

Randy

Num. 6:24-26

BOB JONES
UNIVERSITY PRESS

Greenville, South Carolina

Library of Congress Cataloging-in-Publication Data

Leedy, Randy, 1960-
   Love not the world : winning the war against worldliness / Randy Leedy.
      p. cm.
   Summary: "An exposition of the biblical concepts of the world and worldliness"—Provided by publisher.
   Includes bibliographical references.
   ISBN 978-1-60682-041-4 (perfect bound pbk. : alk. paper)
   1. Church and the world. 2. Christianity—Philosophy. 3. Christian philosophy. 4. Worldliness. I. Title.
   BR115.W6L399 2012
   241—dc23

                                                                    2011051720

Love Not the World: Winning the War against Worldliness
Randy Leedy, PhD

Design and page layout by Nathan Hutcheon

© 2012 by BJU Press
Greenville, South Carolina 29614

Bob Jones University Press is a division of BJU Press

Printed in the United States of America
All rights reserved

ISBN 978-1-60682-041-4

15   14   13   12   11   10   9   8   7   6   5   4   3   2   1

Dedicated to Homer Francis Vian (1926-2012).

When as a young man my father was drifting downward, dismissive of the gospel because of the hypocrisy of worldly Christians, Homer's self-sacrificing love modeled the life-changing power of true discipleship and drew him to Christ. Knowing my flesh to the extent that I do, I shudder to think where I would be today and for eternity had Homer, too, loved the world more than the Savior.

Homer, when I join you in glory, I pray that our Father will show me some special way to express how much I love you. Here and now, may He use this book to increase your tribe!

CONTENTS

INTRODUCTION

"See that thou lovest," advised William Penn, "what is lovely."[1] Echoing biblical wisdom (Phil. 4:8), Penn warns against misplaced affection. Our sinful world dangles lovely promises of delight before our pleasure-seeking eyes, wooing us with an all-but-irresistible seduction. Nor are those promises entirely false. Embracing them yields just enough pleasure, for just long enough, to ensnare and enslave us in rebellion against the Creator and Lover of our souls. Our Father's warning, then, "Love not the world" (1 John 2:15), robs us of no rightful, fruitful joy. If the world (in this evil sense of the word) were lovely, it would deserve our love. But since it only pretends to be lovely, it deserves to be unmasked and its ugliness displayed, that we may learn, through Spirit-empowered self-denial, to hate it.

"Love not the world." Our Father wastes none of His words; He issues no unnecessary warnings. He warns against loving the world because He knows that even His own people strongly incline to do just that.

But do we recognize that propensity, not just among others but also—or even especially—within *ourselves*? It would be a fascinating study for a professional pollster to survey members and attendees of Bible-believing churches, asking two questions. First, what percentage of the people within your Bible-believing circles do

---

[1] William Penn, *Some Fruits of Solitude,* in *Reflections and Maxims Relating to the Conduct of Human Life* (London: T. Northcott, 1693), §79 (p. 28). In context, Penn's meaning is not "See that you *do* love what is lovely," but "See that you love *only* what is lovely."

you consider worldly? Second, do you consider yourself worldly? While I have never attempted both questions of such a survey, everyone to whom I mention the idea here at Bob Jones University and at my local church agrees that the responses would almost certainly show that we see more worldliness in others than we see in ourselves. I did put the first question to a BJU Seminary class of about twenty-five students. Their answers varied from 10 percent to 90 percent, averaging around 50 percent. When I wondered aloud what the responses to the second question would be, had I posed it, the class agreed that few if any would identify themselves as worldly. How can half of us be worldly if hardly any of us are worldly?

This disconnect between how we view others and how we view ourselves is not surprising. Sociologist Sinikka Elliott, in an in-depth study of about sixty-five parents, found a very strong pattern of parents' thinking that their own teenagers are much less sexually active than other teens are.[2] Similarly, a 2011 survey of 848 U.S. drivers found 64 percent of respondents rating themselves as "excellent" or "very good" drivers, while placing less than 30 percent of others, even their close friends, in those categories.[3] Among the variety of explanations for this phenomenon must lie the fallen human instinct to assume the best about ourselves. Do you remember the lawyer in Luke 10, whose question "And who is my neighbour?" prompts Jesus to tell the story of the Good Samaritan? Perhaps you've never noticed that Luke records the

---

[2] Martha Waggoner, "Parents Don't Believe Their Kids Have Sex." The Associated Press wire story, dated June 16, 2010, is posted at http://abcnews.go.com/Entertainment/wirestory?id=10930698&page=1, accessed July 6, 2010. Elliott's forthcoming book *Not My Kid: Parents and Teen Sexuality* will be published by New York University Press (expected in 2012).

[3] http://www.allstatenewsroom.com/channels/News-Releases/releases/new-allstate-survey-shows-americans-think-they-are-great-drivers-habits-tell-a-different-story, accessed November 5, 2011.

motivation behind that question: the lawyer wants to justify himself (Luke 10:29). He wants to think of himself as having done what is necessary to inherit eternal life, and he knows that the law requires him to love his neighbor as himself. Of course, he has not loved his neighbor as himself—if he is honest, he will admit that, like the priest and the Levite in Jesus' story, he has miserably failed. Yet he thinks himself righteous, and he believes he can confirm that status if he can get Jesus to confirm his definition of *neighbor*, which in his mind was no doubt a relatively small group (cf. Matt. 5:43). Where did he learn such a pattern of reasoning? It extends all the way back to Genesis 3, where Adam and Eve manifested the sinner's instinctive reluctance to admit failure openly before God. The flesh always thinks it is better than it is.

Our fleshly tendency toward self-satisfaction applies as well to the confidence with which we hold our lifestyle preferences. Without searching the Scriptures in a self-examining way, we tend to assume that God agrees with us, forgetful of a coming day of accountability at the Judgment Seat of Christ (Rom. 14:12; 2 Cor. 5:10).

Let's pursue that prospect for a moment. Imagine yourself standing in Christ's awesome, glorified presence—the presence that invariably caused those who experienced it on earth to fall at His feet as though dead. He asks, "Why, when you were living on earth, did you do such and such?" While every honest Christian readily confesses that not all his actions and habits stem from worthy motives, surely every healthy conscience testifies that only one explanation deserves a hearing before the Sovereign of all: "Lord, I honestly believed I was obeying Your Word." Nothing is more important to the believer in the process of making life's decisions than a deliberate submission to the Word of God, coupled with as clear as possible an understanding of what the Scripture teaches on the matter at issue.

Few if any Bible believers, of course, will disagree with the previous paragraph in theory. Given the observable realities of the prevailing modes of Christian living, though, I suspect—and even hope—that more than a few who read this book will, by the end, be inclined to take me for a fool. Many of the Corinthian believers manifested an inclination, common to every place and time, to prize worldly wisdom. So it was to us as well as to them that Paul offered strong correction: "If any man among you seemeth to be wise in this world, let him become a fool, that he may be wise. For the wisdom of this world is foolishness with God" (1 Cor. 3:18*b*–19). If God has enabled me to express His wisdom on the topic of worldliness, then to the worldly wise I will seem a fool.

Of course, my hope does not end with being taken for a fool. If those so inclined will also heed Paul's corrective, they will humble themselves before the Word of God and join the holy band in what the world sees as foolishness. There is no other path to the wisdom of God that today's church so desperately needs.

A helpful body of literature on the topic of worldliness has developed in recent decades as observers of Evangelicalism have noted and, in some cases, become alarmed at the degree to which prevailing secular morality has invaded their movement. These books, though dealing primarily with broader Evangelicalism, are worth the attention of fundamentalists as well, since our own movement lags not far behind Evangelicalism in its assimilation of popular culture and seems to be rapidly closing the gap.[4]

---

[4] A few of the more prominent titles include Richard Quebedeaux, *The Worldly Evangelicals* (San Francisco: Harper and Row, 1978); James Davison Hunter, *Evangelicalism: The Coming Generation* (Chicago: University of Chicago Press, 1987); R. Kent

Why another book, when such helpful literature already exists and so far seems to have failed to make much impact on layman-level Christian living? One justification is that a lack of Fundamentalist voices raised against encroaching worldliness would constitute a signal failure of spiritual leadership within our movement. We can be thankful that many calls for holiness are arising from separatist pulpits and in the various electronic media, and the chorus ought to swell within the traditional print media as well. Fundamentalist leaders need publications that they can recommend with few if any disclaimers about either the content of the work or the associations of the author.

Another reason for this book is an important gap in the current literature. Titles such as those listed in footnote 4 do a good job of surveying the character of the ecclesiastical scene, describing and quantifying shifts in attitudes and practices among individuals in recent years, and warning against specific manifestations of worldliness in various matters of philosophy and lifestyle such as worldview, music and entertainment, use of money, fashion, Lord's Day observance, and sexuality, marriage, and family life. What appears to remain lacking is a reasonably well-developed biblical theology of the world and worldliness. This is not to say that the literature on the topic fails to uphold the Scripture. The works reflecting the greatest degree of alarm (such as those by Hughes and Mahaney, mentioned in footnote 4) do emphasize biblical instruction, both that which is general (e.g., "Love not the world") and that which is more specific (e.g., "Flee fornication"). But beyond offering a definition of the world such as "the organized system of human civilization that is actively hostile to God and alienated from

---

Hughes, *Set Apart: Calling a Worldly Church to a Godly Life* (Wheaton, IL: Crossway, 2003); and C. J. Mahaney, ed., *Worldliness: Resisting the Seduction of a Fallen World* (Wheaton, IL: Crossway, 2008).

God,"[5] these works do not seem to develop the Bible's full portrait of the world in adequate detail, nor do they adequately explore the Old Testament foundations for the New Testament's warnings against worldliness. This is not to fault these authors; their purposes in writing simply did not provide space for such discussion.

This lack of theological development is one of the reasons for the degree of disagreement and misunderstanding that currently prevails. To the extent that our understanding of the scriptural revelation on these topics is incomplete, we will likely fail to identify the world accurately and to keep our lives pure from its corruption. Our partial understandings then generate conflict as we each err differently from others. None of the Lord's servants has anything to say, on this or any other topic, that will truly help God's people until they have first learned what God has already said. Only then can they convey that truth accurately and customize it to their hearers or readers with appropriate application. Otherwise, they are merely blind leaders of the blind.

A fully developed biblical theology of the world and worldliness, though, is much too large an undertaking for this single small volume. Except perhaps for the sections of extended genealogy, hardly a page of Scripture lacks information relevant to the topic. Nevertheless, substantial coverage is possible, especially if the focus remains primarily[6] on passages where the actual terminology for

---

[5] Mahaney, 26.

[6] The word *primarily* is important. This study does not restrict itself exclusively to passages using the various words for the world; numerous passages including the idea but lacking the specific vocabulary contribute to its development. Psalm 1:1 would be a good example: "Blessed is the man that walketh not in the counsel of the ungodly." The only sense in which the study underlying this book has been comprehensive, though, is that I have considered all of the hundreds of passages that use the key words for "the world."

the world appears. The body of texts containing this vocabulary is large enough to provide sufficient exposure to the range of biblical teaching on the topic.

Along with this focus on biblical teaching, we must also pursue contemporary application. Here, too, we will devote our attention to issues that have not yet been fully developed in the literature on worldliness. Jumping too quickly into specific applications will immediately generate controversy among those who differ on the question of which areas of life are in fact subject to the possibility of worldliness. Scriptural teaching on matters of style in music and personal grooming, for example, is less than clear, direct, and comprehensive. Paul did not directly address the issue of attendance at the Roman theatre of his day. Some will conclude from such omissions that music, entertainment, and grooming are matters on which our Father extends to us the full liberty of personal preference. Others will sense in such matters a cultural significance that they believe warrants bringing them under the Bible's general admonitions regarding worldliness. Such differences suggest that we will do well to think carefully about the question of application in general, as an issue in itself, before taking up the specific issues on which the convictions, preferences, and—dare I suggest it?—loves we have already formed are likely to distort our judgment and prevent objective evaluation.

Prerequisite, then, to our ability to grasp and obey the Lord's instruction regarding worldliness is a thorough grounding in the two major thrusts of this book: the Bible's general teaching on the nature of the world and the believer's relationship to it, and principles to guide our application of this teaching to specific aspects of our lives. While specific application of this biblical teaching to various issues is not completely absent, extended development of such discussion must await other publishing opportunities.

Before moving on to the main body of the work, let's have a little chat regarding that detestable word *legalism*. A writer who emphasizes scriptural obligations requiring self-denial is sure to be dismissed by some as a legalist. "Graceless," they will call his work. I hope that the content of this book will provoke no such reaction from fair-minded readers. But, regardless, I wish to deny emphatically, here at the outset, any charge of legalism.

Though the word *legalism* does not appear in the Bible, it is a fair label for certain uses of God's commands that Scripture portrays and rejects.[7] Luke's Gospel portrays two quintessential legalists: the Pharisee whose self-congratulating prayer expresses thanks that he is so obedient in comparison to the sinners around him (18:9–14), and the elder brother who angrily reminds his father of his lifelong, unwavering obedience in contrast to his brother's profligacy (15:29ff.), completely unaware of how deeply his conduct at that very moment, as he vents his hatred, dishonors and grieves his father. Luke captures the essence of both men's error when he introduces the Pharisee with this description: "Certain which trusted in themselves that they were righteous, and despised others" (18:9).

One of the marks of a legalist is that he loves rules so that he can keep them and then congratulate himself on his success. Loving rules, though, is not in itself a mark of a legalist. David loved God's rules: "I love thy commandments above gold"; "My soul hath kept thy testimonies; and I love them exceedingly" (Ps. 119:127, 167). And of course Jesus kept His Father's commandments and always did what pleased Him (John 8:29; 15:10). But David's and Jesus'

---

[7] For further discussion, see Ken Casillas, *The Law and the Christian: God's Light within God's Limits* (Greenville: Bob Jones University Press, 2007) and Randy Jaeggli, *Love, Liberty, and Christian Conscience: Striking the Biblical Balance* (Greenville: Bob Jones University Press, 2007).

obedience was not self-righteous. It was rather their wise, proper, and heartfelt response to God's benevolent authority and to the inherent rightness and value of His commands. Rightly motivated obedience based on wise understanding is not legalism!

An illustration will make the distinction clear. Imagine a hospital where specific procedures are required for health and safety matters such as sterilization of surgical instruments, disposal of sharp objects, hand washing, handling and disposal of chemicals, and cleaning of the facility. The complete set of rules fills many pages. Now imagine four employees. Two of them are careful to follow all procedures. They regularly review them so they don't forget, and they remind and prompt one another when they observe infractions. One of them, though, doesn't relate to patients well, often displaying rudeness and insensitivity, while the other is warm and caring toward all. Eventually the root difference between them becomes apparent: the rude one doesn't care about patient welfare. He just thinks that his job performance is going to be evaluated in terms of his adherence to policy, so he keeps the rules in order to earn a reputation as a model employee, expecting salary increases and promotions. The other keeps the rules out of a genuine care for the welfare of the patients, and her care manifests itself in many ways beyond the rule-keeping. Only the first, of course, is a legalist.

The third employee is different. He doesn't hide his disdain for the rules and the patients. He works as little as possible and grumbles constantly. The fourth employee just enjoys people and loves to carry on with the patients and the other workers. She has a general idea about the procedures and doesn't really reject them, but she doesn't worry much about the details as she moves from one conversation to the next throughout the day. These two employees' relationship with the legalist, who always looks down his nose at them, consists largely of fending off his reports to the boss for insufficient adherence to procedure. The truly caring employee, fearing for the patients' welfare, also encourages these two to be more careful.

How many legalists do you suppose the two lax employees think they work with? Probably two. Their unconcern for health and safety is evidence that they don't fully understand the realities of their situation. It is no surprise, then, if they also fail to perceive the difference in motivation between the two rule-keepers who so often ruin their day.

This book does not push for keeping rules for the sake of some self-deceived sense of superiority. The most obedient "elder brother" is made of the same flesh as his most "prodigal" brothers and sisters. Rather, this book is a plea for all of us who love the Lord to put our heads and hearts together in a careful searching of the Scriptures to pursue a clear understanding of the direction our Father has given us about the realities of our situation and how to handle them. Our culture is full of deadly toxins and pathogens, and dangerous instruments and situations.[8] The desire to understand and then diligently and methodically to act always in the interest of health and safety, to the glory of God, is what I trust will emerge as the spirit of this book. This is not legalism!

---

[8] Included among the death-dealing influences to be found within our culture is legalism itself. The fact that the legalists came in for Jesus' harshest criticism indicates that, of the three spiritual states represented by the three inferior employees in the illustration, God may well see legalism as the worst. To a prospective patient, a "legalistically clean" hospital may not sound so bad, but we must remember that illustrations are always limited. If legalism is spiritually toxic or pathogenic itself, then there is no such thing as being legalistically clean. The Pharisees' external purity only masked the abominations that festered in their hearts (Matt. 23:25–28; Luke 16:15). The fact that one error is the worst, however, does not justify the other two. The two who are lax about the procedures cannot justify their laxity by saying, "You should be happy I'm not a legalist!"

Nor is it gracelessness, in the sense of the saving grace revealed in Scripture. According to Titus 2:11–12 and Romans 6:1, anything called grace that provides safe haven for ungodliness and worldly lust, or that condones continuing in sin, is something other than the saving grace of Christ. Such perverted grace (cf. Jude 4), I trust, is absent from the pages of this book.

Please infer from this self-defense no claim to perfection. I have labored constantly under the ambivalence of delight at the rich truths this study has enabled me to savor and regret over the awareness that my best efforts in writing fall short of the glory with which such truths deserve to be expressed. So, with no unrealistic expectation of theological impeccability or of airtight conclusions regarding the Christian's posture toward every aspect of contemporary culture, but with holy desire to learn and conform ourselves to divine wisdom, let us take up our task.

Complicating that task is the fact that careful examination of the text of Scripture is not a popular activity in many Fundamentalist circles today. Our culture no longer conditions us, if it ever did, for the labor of careful and accurate reading. With this fact in mind, I have invested extensive effort in making the biblical teaching as easy as possible to understand. And as understanding materializes, interest rises—how can a child of God fail to find his Father's conversation interesting? But the reader must also assume a share of responsibility to exert effort in pursuit of understanding. May I ask you to pray sincerely for our Father's enabling to understand what He has revealed to you in His Word? He spoke with the intent to be understood. In dependence upon God, I am writing with the intent to help you understand. If you will read with that same intent and that same dependence, I believe that God will bless you with the understanding you seek, perhaps greater understanding than you even knew to desire. If I did not believe this, I would have no heart to risk writing on such a controversial theme.

1

DEFINING THE WORLD, PART 1:
OLD TESTAMENT FOUNDATIONS

A study of any topic must begin by defining its terms. Only one term concerns us at the moment: *world*. A full and precise definition appears later, but we need at least a simple one to work with at the outset. Most readers will already have noticed that I have used the word *world* without stating which of several possible senses I intend. For example, in the sentences "God created the world in six days" and "The world hates God," the meaning is obviously not the same. Most readers will have understood already that I am using *world* as in that second sentence: the lost people of our generation, especially as they manifest their estrangement from our Father by developing and pursuing values that are contrary to the biblical morality that reflects His character. So this book is not about the world in the sense of the physical earth or its animal and human inhabitants considered without respect to their morality. It is about those aspects of human culture in which unbelievers manifest their rejection of and hostility toward God.

This description of the world requires us to establish with clarity the relationship between the world and culture. *Culture* is simply the set of patterns of thought, communication, and behavior shared by a group of people living together as a society. It results from the natural human tendency to imitate what we observe in others, and without it social harmony would be impossible. Culture, then, unlike the world as described above, is something to respect and value. Cultural patterns, however, are not always good. Human cultures are sinners' cultures, featuring various forms of sinfulness. Scripture shines upon culture the light of truth and holiness, enabling us to evaluate the moral character of a given culture's various elements. Differences in culture across boundaries of place, language, and time make such evaluation challenging, but the Scripture's guidance is sufficient. The aspects of culture approved by Scripture are to be embraced; those rejected are to be shunned. Of course, some aspects of a culture may not receive definitive evaluation in Scripture; these are the cases where our task is most difficult. The scripturally rejected aspects of a given culture are what we may call the world within that society; John Frame has defined it most simply: "*World* is the bad part of culture."[1]

When I write *culture*, then, without a qualifying adjective, I generally intend no more than a mildly negative connotation. *Popular culture* especially refers to contemporary culture as developed and propagated through the mass media. To gain the audience they need in order to survive, the mass media tend to appeal to sinful lusts, so I use that expression more negatively than *culture*. *World*, of course, is entirely negative, with no redeeming virtues. Now let us move on to the Scriptures.

The study of any Bible theme must always begin in the Old Testament, where our Father lays the foundations on which New Testament revelation rests. This particular study immediately faces a challenge in that the word *world* is not especially common in most English versions of the Old Testament. It occurs forty-six times

---

[1] John Frame, *The Doctrine of the Christian Life* (Phillipsburg, NJ: P&R Publishing, 2008), 866. Kevin Bauder makes the same point in a Central Baptist Theological Seminary chapel message, available at http://www.centralseminary.edu/resources/mp3-audio/147-understanding-worldliness-a-biblical-investigation-part-4. Accessed June 21, 2010. Though Bauder occasionally seems to express an unhelpful disdain toward some of the past generation's convictions, the whole five-part series is nevertheless well worth hearing.

in the King James Version, and between forty and sixty times in most others. Certainly those are enough occurrences to provide a fruitful study, but it is doubtful whether *any* of those occurrences carries the sense that is relevant for our study. The best candidate is Psalm 17:14, which speaks of "men of the world, which have their portion in this life." Next best are several verses that speak of God's judging the world (Ps. 9:8; 96:13; 98:9), but there is no reason to restrict the reference of *world* to those who do not know God, since *judge* need not be restricted to condemnation and punishment. The great majority of occurrences of *world* in the Old Testament refer to the physical creation or to humanity as a whole, encompassing good and bad—those who know God and those who do not.

"THE NATIONS" IN THE OLD TESTAMENT

The fact that the Old Testament does not use *world* much, if at all, in the sense that concerns us in this book[2] does not mean, though, that the idea of lost humanity in rebellion against the Father does not appear in the Old Testament. In the Old Testament economy, at least from Abraham on, God largely restricted His special revelation to His chosen nation, Israel. The mass of people alienated from and hostile to the Lord were "the nations."[3] This Hebrew expression and its New Testament Greek equivalent[4] are often translated in the King James Version as "the Gentiles" or "the heathen": the segment of humanity outside the nation Israel. So the nearest Old Testament expression for "the world" in our sense is "the

---

[2] The statement is as true for the Hebrew words referring to the earth (the most common of which are *'eretz* and *tebel*) as it is for the English *world*.

[3] The Hebrew words are הַגּוֹיִם (*hagoyim*) or, less commonly, הָעַמִּים (*ha'ammim*, "the peoples").

[4] ἔθνη (*ethne*).

nations," and the nearest Old Testament expression for the concept of conformity to the world is being like the nations.

A perusal of the roughly seven hundred Old Testament occurrences of the Hebrew expressions for "the nations" and "the peoples"[5] uncovers a theme with fascinating development. Not all of these occurrences feature the idea of "the world" that this book develops; many or perhaps even most of them lack, or at least do not feature, the moral component of rebellion against God. But we must sketch the broad picture in order to have the clearest background against which to perceive the teaching of the Old Testament about the nations in that "worldly" sense.

Early in Genesis our Father records the division of humanity into nations, putting the verb in the passive voice. "By these were the isles of the Gentiles divided in their lands; every one after his tongue, after their families, in their nations" (Gen. 10:5), and, "These are the families of the sons of Noah, after their generations, in their nations: and by these were the nations divided in the earth after the flood" (Gen. 10:32). Who made these divisions?[6] The very next verse begins the account of how the nations were divided, and our Father is the active agent as He confuses the language of the people at Babel, thus scattering them across the inhabitable earth (Gen. 11:1–9). Our Father, then, is the One Who

---

[5] Those who wish to approximate this list of occurrences with a computer search of the English Old Testament will get the most accurate results by searching for *nations, peoples,* or *Gentiles* in the American Standard Version, the New American Standard Bible, or the English Standard Version. The King James Version matches the Hebrew less closely because it translates the Hebrew plural for "the peoples" with the English singular *people* much more often that the other versions do. The same search, though, with the addition of *heathen,* in the King James Version does yield the majority of important passages related to the theme of "the nations" in the Old Testament.

[6] The phrase "by these" in this context does not indicate the agent who does the action, as in, "The students were divided into groups by the teacher." Instead it indicates the criterion on which the division was based, as in, "The students were divided into groups by their favorite sport."

created the nations, not only in the sense of His having created the human race, but also in the sense of His imposing divisions into national entities with their linguistic, geographical, and cultural differences. Deuteronomy confirms this truth when Moses declares to Israel that God has placed her "above all nations which he hath made" (26:19), and again when he writes, "When the most High divided to the nations their inheritance, when he separated the sons of Adam, he set the bounds of the people according to the number of the children of Israel" (32:8).

So the origin of the nations is the creative and controlling hand of God, motivated by wise purposes. What will be their end? In reply to this question we find different answers in Scripture. Israel's end, of course, is immeasurable blessing. What, though, of the other nations? In some passages we read that particular Gentile nations, or the nations in general, are destined for destruction. This is especially true of the Canaanite nations, whose abominable immorality marked them for extermination at the hand of the Israelites, whom God would lead in conquest over them in fulfillment of His promises to Abraham, Isaac, and Jacob. That destruction is indeed complete. Israel has survived the wrath of the nations for millennia, but where in the world today could you find a community of Canaanites, Hittites, Amorites, Perizzites, Hivites, Girgashites or Jebusites?

The same destiny awaits every godless nation: "The wicked shall be turned into hell, and all the nations that forget God" (Ps. 9:17). Perhaps the Old Testament's most impressive passage about the eventual destruction of all the godless nations is the prophecy of Isaiah 34, especially verses 1–5:

> Come near, ye nations, to hear; and hearken, ye people:
> let the earth hear, and all that is therein; the world, and

all things that come forth of it. For the indignation of the Lord is upon all nations, and his fury upon all their armies: he hath utterly destroyed them, he hath delivered them to the slaughter. Their slain also shall be cast out, and their stink shall come up out of their carcases, and the mountains shall be melted with their blood. And all the host of heaven shall be dissolved, and the heavens shall be rolled together as a scroll: and all their host shall fall down, as the leaf falleth off from the vine, and as a falling fig from the fig tree. For my sword shall be bathed in heaven: behold, it shall come down upon Idumea, and upon the people of my curse, to judgment.

When we find ourselves tempted to walk in the ways of the world, it will be our Savior's mercy to us if as a warning He recalls to our minds what He has said will be the end of those who rebel against Him.

Such warnings of destruction, however, do not comprise the whole of the Old Testament's witness about what the end of the nations will be. The Abrahamic covenant promised blessing for "all families of the earth" (Gen. 12:3). The nations would not have to wait for the Millennium for this blessing, either, for God intended the nation Israel to serve as a testimony to His character:

Behold, I have taught you statutes and judgments, even as the Lord my God commanded me, that ye should do so in the land whither ye go to possess it. Keep therefore and do them; for this is your wisdom and your understanding in the sight of the nations, which shall hear all these statutes, and say, Surely this great nation is a wise and understanding people. For what nation is there so great, who hath God so nigh unto them, as the Lord our God is in all things that we call upon him for? And what nation is there so great, that hath statutes and judgments so righteous as all this law, which I set before you this day? (Deut. 4:5–8).

This intention materialized to some extent in Israel's early history, culminating in Solomon's reign: "And there came of all people to hear the wisdom of Solomon, from all kings of the earth, which had heard of his wisdom" (1 Kings 4:34). Likewise Solomon's prayer at the dedication of the temple reflected Israel's role as a testimony to the nations:

> Moreover concerning a stranger, that is not of thy people Israel, but cometh out of a far country for thy name's sake; (for they shall hear of thy great name, and of thy strong hand, and of thy stretched out arm;) when he shall come and pray toward this house; hear thou in heaven thy dwelling place, and do according to all that the stranger calleth to thee for: that all people of the earth may know thy name, to fear thee, as do thy people Israel; and that they may know that this house, which I have builded, is called by thy name (1 Kings 8:41–43).

Only in the Millennium, though, does the Abrahamic blessing extend fully to all the nations. Given our tendency to view the Old Testament's prophecies of blessing as intended only for the Jews and, by extension, for New Testament saints as a spiritual rather than a national body, passages like the following, when we give them even a moment's meditation, are truly breathtaking. In a messianic prophecy, God declared to His Son, "It is a light thing that thou shouldest be my servant to raise up the tribes of Jacob, and to restore the preserved of Israel: I will also give thee for a light to the Gentiles, that thou mayest be my salvation unto the end of the earth" (Isa. 49:6). And, unlike current experience in most

19

evangelistic work, this offer of salvation will not go neglected, for the Lord promises His Messiah, "The Gentiles shall come to thy light, and kings to the brightness of thy rising" (Isa. 60:3). This salvation will transform the nations completely: "At that time they shall call Jerusalem the throne of the Lord; and all the nations shall be gathered unto it, to the name of the Lord, to Jerusalem: neither shall they walk any more after the imagination of their evil heart" (Jer. 3:17). Micah is even more specific, promising that the Messiah "shall judge among many people,[7] and rebuke strong nations afar off; and they shall beat their swords into plowshares, and their spears into pruninghooks: nation shall not lift up a sword against nation, neither shall they learn war any more" (Mic. 4:3). Two prophecies of Zechariah are especially warm in their relational tone: "Many nations shall be joined to the Lord in that day, and shall be my people" (Zech. 2:11*a*), and, my personal favorite, "He shall speak peace unto the heathen: and his dominion shall be from sea even to sea, and from the river even to the ends of the earth" (9:10).

How is it, though, that Scripture can speak in such opposite terms? "The indignation of the Lord is upon all nations," Isaiah declares, while Zechariah promises, "He shall speak peace unto the heathen." Psalm 9:17 seems to hold the key: "The wicked shall be turned into hell, and all the nations that forget God." Once Jesus Christ takes the throne of David for His Millennial reign, the nations will no longer be able to forget God, and their submission to the Son will bring upon them the rich blessings promised throughout the Old Testament.

---

[7] "People" in the Hebrew text is plural, "peoples."

Our Father's ultimate intent for all nations, then, is to pour out upon them the Abrahamic blessing, but first He must deal out destruction in retribution for their rebellion against Him.

Israel among the Nations

Within this overall framework of God's dealings with the nations, the Old Testament also reveals the Great Shepherd's dealings with the single nation, Israel, that He establishes as the channel through which the Abrahamic blessing would flow to the ends of the earth. Like all the other nations, Israel exists because God brought her into being. God's originating work in the case of this nation, though, is unique. While the origin of the Gentile nations appears to be the outcome of the natural and ordinary development of man's race after the confusion of languages at Babel, Israel's origin and development at every stage, especially during her infancy and adolescence, is the product of God's miraculous activity. God first calls Abram (whom He later renames Abraham, "Father of a Multitude") out of his pagan homeland and then, after decades of delay, miraculously enables him and Sarah to produce their first child at an age when reproduction was humanly impossible. In the time of Joseph, God engineers the family's migration to Egypt, where social barriers prevent its assimilation into Egypt[8] while over a period of some four centuries Abraham's family grows into a nation. Then, when the time is right, God works mighty miracles to lead Israel out of Egypt, through the wilderness and into Canaan, which He had promised the patriarchs He would give to their descendants as their land.

---

[8] See Gen. 43:32; 46:34. Though I am not aware that Scripture explicitly mentions it, a likely further purpose of this migration would have been to prevent Israel's assimilation into the abominable culture of the Canaanite nations that God intended to use Israel eventually to eradicate.

In the later stages of this development, as Israel is coming out of Egypt and into Canaan, God speaks often through Moses to teach the people how and why He has brought their nation into existence. Perhaps the most complete statement of this sort appears in Deuteronomy:

> For ask now of the days that are past, which were before thee, since the day that God created man upon the earth, and ask from the one side of heaven unto the other, whether there hath been any such thing as this great thing is, or hath been heard like it? Did ever people hear the voice of God speaking out of the midst of the fire, as thou hast heard, and live? Or hath God assayed to go and take him a nation from the midst of another nation, by temptations, by signs, and by wonders, and by war, and by a mighty hand, and by a stretched out arm, and by great terrors, according to all that the Lord your God did for you in Egypt before your eyes? Unto thee it was shewed, that thou mightest know that the Lord he is God; there is none else beside him. Out of heaven he made thee to hear his voice, that he might instruct thee: and upon earth he shewed thee his great fire; and thou heardest his words out of the midst of the fire. And because he loved thy fathers, therefore he chose their seed after them, and brought thee out in his sight with his mighty power out of Egypt; to drive out nations from before thee greater and mightier than thou art, to bring thee in, to give thee their land for an inheritance, as it is this day. Know therefore this day, and consider it in thine heart, that the Lord he is God in heaven above, and upon the earth beneath: there is none else (Deut. 4:32–39).

Our Father dealt with His chosen people Israel in this way for the purpose of manifesting Himself to them as the true God of all the earth. As we have already seen, though, this benevolent purpose was not intended for Israel's advantage alone; through Israel God spoke to all the nations. Almost certainly this role of Israel as a testimony to the other nations lies behind the statement God gave to Israel when she first arrived at Sinai: "Ye shall be unto me a kingdom of priests, and an holy nation" (Exod. 19:6a). The function of a priest is to mediate between God and man. Is the picture intended here that Israel would be a nation of individuals mediating for one another in their corporate service to God? This is hardly possible; after all, God selected Levi as the one priestly tribe within the nation. Not all Israelites were entitled to function equally as priests. Rather, God intended that this nation as a unit would serve as a priest among the nations, to testify to them the same truth that Israel's existence declares to the chosen nation itself: Jehovah,[9] God of Israel, is the one and only true God (Deut. 4:35, 39).

Old Testament history records, though, only a modicum of success by Israel in this role. At the time of the Exodus and the conquest of Canaan, the nations indeed feared Israel and her God, but, with occasional exceptions such as Rahab and the Gibeonites, they did not submit. What went wrong? Part of the problem, perhaps the biggest part, lay with Israel's failure to meet God's conditions. The verse preceding God's promise that Israel would be a kingdom of priests and a holy nation conditions that role on Israel's obedience to His commands: "Now therefore, if ye will obey my voice indeed, and keep my covenant" (Exod. 19:5a). Israel did not obey,

---

[9] It is widely understood that a more accurate representation of the divine name in English letters would be *Yahweh*. In the interest of using language familiar to most readers, though, I will use the more traditional *Jehovah*.

and in her disobedience she forfeited much of her ability to serve as a testimony of God's greatness to the Gentiles.

Why, though, did Israel disobey? Surely she did not intend to disobey. Scripture records repeated national commitments to obedience, beginning with the Exodus 19 passage under discussion here (Exod. 19:8; 24:3, 7; Deut. 5:27; 26:17; Josh. 24:1–28, esp. v. 24). Scripture does not leave us guessing about why Israel disobeyed. The root of Israel's disobedience was not disaffection with God; it was affection for the ways of the nations. Israel did not wake up one morning with a sudden resentment against God; rather, she increasingly pursued her appetite for the fleshly ways of her pagan neighbors. The true God did not alienate His people by some harsh action toward them;[10] rather, the false gods of the nations wooed Israel's attention away from all that her own Shepherd had provided and promised.

This appetite for the ways of the nations afflicted the family of Abraham from the beginning. Lot was the first to succumb, and Esau was another early victim. Jacob's sons were no testimony of righteousness in their generation, with the bright exception of Joseph. Within just a few weeks after the Lord miraculously delivered Israel from the Egyptians at the Red Sea, the people were longing for their old Egyptian diet (Exod. 16:2–3). And when Moses and Aaron were on Sinai receiving the law, the people quickly degenerated into Egyptian idolatry featuring debauched worship of a golden calf, and their piously calling it a feast to Jehovah cleansed none of its corruption (Exod. 32:4–7). Stephen's sermon in Acts 7 describes this phase of Israel's history in these tragic terms: "In their hearts [they] turned back again into Egypt" (Acts 7:39).

---

[10] To test her faith and obedience, God did allow Israel to suffer hardship.

The giving of the Mosaic law in all its detail, coupled with Israel's promises to obey, did not solve the problem. Achan brought defeat upon the nation by his lust for money and fine clothing (Josh. 7:21). At the end of Joshua's life, just one generation into Israel's residency in Canaan, idolatry was again (or perhaps *still*) prevalent. Joshua admonished, "Put away the gods which your fathers served on the other side of the flood, and in Egypt; and serve ye the Lord" (Josh. 24:14), and, "Now therefore put away . . . the strange gods which are among you, and incline your heart unto the Lord God of Israel" (v. 23). The thunderings at Sinai compelled from Israel an intent to obey, but the attractions offered by the nations were simply too much for her to resist.

The Old Testament account of Israel's desire to be like the nations is sobering to contemplate. This desire did not take God by surprise; from the beginning our Father understood its power and what its effects would be. While Israel was still in the wilderness, God anticipated the time when she would say, "I will set a king over me, like as all the nations that are about me" (Deut. 17:14*b*). God goes on to list some stipulations for that king, including warnings about what disobedience will bring (vv. 15–20). Israel's subsequent history, of course, vindicates all those warnings, as every one of those ill effects of disobedience did in fact materialize. But such commands and warnings were not merely for kings: the Father warns the whole nation, "When thou art come into the land which the Lord thy God giveth thee, thou shalt not learn to do after the abominations of those nations" (Deut. 18:9). To behave like the nations, and especially to serve their gods, will bring upon Israel the same destruction that Israel is about to inflict upon the Canaanites:

> And it shall be, if thou do at all forget the Lord thy God, and walk after other gods, and serve them, and worship them, I testify against you this day that ye shall surely perish. As the nations which the Lord destroyeth before your face, so shall ye perish; because ye would not be obedient unto the voice of the Lord your God (Deut. 8:19–20).

This is of course exactly what happened. After about eight centuries of varying degrees of Israel's covenant breaking, the whole nation was dispossessed of its land and either killed, deported to foreign lands, or subjugated under foreign empires while continuing to occupy the Promised Land. God's chosen nation ceased to exist as a nation. The historical books leave no doubt about what failure of Israel's brought about this calamity. 2 Kings 17 records the fall of the Northern Kingdom, offering among the words of explanation these statements:

> For so it was, that the children of Israel had sinned against the Lord their God, . . . and walked in the statutes of the heathen, whom the Lord cast out from before the children of Israel (vv. 7–8).

> And there they burnt incense in all the high places, as did the heathen (v. 11*a*).

> And they rejected his statutes, and his covenant that he made with their fathers, . . . and went after the heathen that were round about them, concerning whom the Lord had charged them, that they should not do like them (v. 15).

The Southern Kingdom suffered the same fate for the same reason:

26

Moreover all the chief of the priests, and the people, transgressed very much after all the abominations of the heathen; and polluted the house of the Lord which he had hallowed in Jerusalem. And the Lord God of their fathers sent to them by his messengers, rising up betimes, and sending; because he had compassion on his people, and on his dwelling place: but they mocked the messengers of God, and despised his words, and misused his prophets, until the wrath of the Lord arose against his people, till there was no remedy (2 Chron. 36:14–16).

Israel's downfall, then, was her appetite to live like the nations.

Of all the aspects of Gentile culture, the one that the Old Testament singles out as the chief temptation for Israel, and the one that represented the most serious breach of Israel's covenant with Jehovah, was the worship of false gods. The first two of the Ten Commandments stipulated that Israel was to have no other God than Jehovah, nor was she to create images to be used even in the worship of the true God. The rationale for these commands, God explained, was that He had entered into a unique, exclusive relationship with Israel: "I am the Lord thy God" (Exod. 20:2), and "I, the Lord thy God" (v. 5). In the previous chapter Israel's Deliverer had declared that, by redeeming her from bondage, He had made her His own (Exod. 19:4), and that she could seal this relationship by obedience to His covenant. It is the same mutual relationship that the hymn writer picked up in penning, "I am His, and He is mine." For Israel to worship other gods, then, is spiritual adultery, a charge God registers frequently against His people throughout the pages of the prophets in particular. Isaiah takes up the topic at the outset of his prophecy. Even oxen and donkeys know their owners, but somehow Israel has fallen away from her God (Isa. 1:3–4). "How is the faithful city become an harlot!" God exclaims

(Isa. 1:21). Hosea's whole prophecy revolves around God's dealings with His adulterous wife. Further, Ezekiel 16, the longest chapter in that book, delivers an especially picturesque and scathing denunciation of Israel's unfaithfulness to her loyal Husband.

Ezekiel 16, in fact, charges Israel with an almost unbelievable degree of spiritual failure. She has actually gone deeper into depravity than the heathen. The harlots of the world at least receive a fee for their services, but Israel has turned things around and pays her customers to gratify her (v. 33). Later in the chapter, God compares Jerusalem to Samaria (the capital of the northern Kingdom, already in captivity) and even Sodom, declaring that Jerusalem has sinned worse than either: "As I live, saith the Lord God, Sodom thy sister hath not done, she nor her daughters, as thou hast done, thou and thy daughters" (v. 48), and, "Neither hath Samaria committed half of thy sins; but thou hast multiplied thine abominations more than they" (v. 51*a*). This emphasis is not unique to Ezekiel; 2 Kings 21:9 and 2 Chronicles 33:9 both declare that Manasseh led the people of Judah into worse sin than the heathen nations that the Lord had driven out at the time of Israel's conquest of Canaan.

God had chosen this nation as His very own. He had commanded her to reflect His own holiness by being like Himself and unlike the nations in morals and religion. In doing so, He promised, Israel would position herself as the object of His richest blessing. He would exalt her high above the nations, and all would marvel at His greatness manifest through her to the entire world. However, the reality that materialized within the Old Testament period was just the opposite. By refusing her Deliverer's covenant, Israel placed herself under His judgment. As a result, Jeremiah laments after the destruction of Jerusalem, "Thou hast made us as the offscouring and refuse in the midst of the people"[11] (Lam. 3:45), and Israel became an object of ridicule among the nations: "Thou makest us a byword among the heathen, a shaking of the head among the people" (Ps. 44:14). Ezekiel uses perhaps the starkest language, where God's charge against Israel is that "they profaned [His] holy name" (Ezek. 36:20).

Ultimately, though, the promise of the Old Testament is that another big reversal is yet to come. In Ezekiel 20, we find Israel's God recounting the broad outline of the history we have been discussing. But this recitation is not delivered in the tones of classroom instruction. Rather, the elders of Israel have come to Ezekiel to inquire of the Lord, and, refusing to answer, the gracious God of heaven launches into a scathing denunciation:

> Ezekiel, tell the elders of Israel that this is what I have to say to them. "Do you come to consult with me? I swear to you that I will not consult with you, because of your abominations. When I swore an oath to Israel in the land of Egypt and promised to bring them into a land flowing with milk and honey, the best of all lands, I said, 'Put away your abominable idols; I am Jehovah your God.' But they rebelled and would not obey me. But for my name's sake, that it might not be defiled in the eyes of the nations, I brought them out of Egypt, and gave them laws—laws that are such as to insure a man's life. But they rebelled against me and rejected my laws. I would have poured out my anger on them, but I refrained in order to keep my name from being defiled in the eyes of the nations. Still, I did not take that generation into the land I had promised, but rather took their children into that land, warning

---

[11] "People" in the Hebrew text is plural, "peoples."

them, too, against disobedience. But they, too, rebelled against me and broke my laws—laws that are such as to insure a man's life. So I let them have laws that were not good—laws that are such as to insure a man's death. I defiled them in their idolatrous worship in order to destroy them, for the purpose that they would know that I am Jehovah." So, Ezekiel, ask the house of Israel, "Are you defiled just like your fathers? Do you commit prostitution just like their abominations? Your pagan worship defiles you with all your idols, to this very day. And should I consult with you, O house of Israel? I swear to you that I will not consult with you!" (Ezek. 20:3–31; author's paraphrase)

At this point in the denunciation, Israel's Great Shepherd makes a startling statement: "And that which cometh into your mind shall not be at all, that ye say, We will be as the heathen, as the families of the countries, to serve wood and stone" (Ezek. 20:32). Here God confronts Israel's stated desire to be like the nations, and He responds flatly, "I'm telling you, it's not going to happen!" Breaking Israel of her imitation of the nations will require stern measures, but in the end God will have His way with His people. Read the remainder of this speech and notice how the tone gradually softens until, at the end, it is downright tender in its accents of repentance (Israel's, of course), forgiveness, and restoration:

> As I live, saith the Lord God, surely with a mighty hand, and with a stretched out arm, and with fury poured out, will I rule over you: and I will bring you out from the people, and will gather you out of the countries wherein ye are scattered, with a mighty hand, and with a stretched out arm, and with fury poured out. And I will bring you

into the wilderness of the people, and there will I plead with you face to face. Like as I pleaded with your fathers in the wilderness of the land of Egypt, so will I plead with you, saith the Lord God. And I will cause you to pass under the rod, and I will bring you into the bond of the covenant: and I will purge out from among you the rebels, and them that transgress against me: I will bring them forth out of the country where they sojourn, and they shall not enter into the land of Israel: and ye shall know that I am the Lord. As for you, O house of Israel, thus saith the Lord God; Go ye, serve ye every one his idols, and hereafter also, if ye will not hearken unto me: but pollute ye my holy name no more with your gifts, and with your idols. For in mine holy mountain, in the mountain of the height of Israel, saith the Lord God, there shall all the house of Israel, all of them in the land, serve me: there will I accept them, and there will I require your offerings, and the firstfruits of your oblations, with all your holy things. I will accept you with your sweet savour, when I bring you out from the people, and gather you out of the countries wherein ye have been scattered; and I will be sanctified in you before the heathen. And ye shall know that I am the Lord, when I shall bring you into the land of Israel, into the country for the which I lifted up mine hand to give it to your fathers. And there shall ye remember your ways, and all your doings, wherein ye have been defiled; and ye shall lothe yourselves in your own sight for all your evils that ye have committed. And ye shall know that I am the Lord, when I have wrought with you for my name's sake, not according to your wicked ways, nor according to your corrupt doings, O ye house of Israel, saith the Lord God (Ezek. 20:33–44).

31

The bottom line of the Old Testament's revelation about Israel's worldliness is that it is only temporary. It costs the nation a heavy price, but God is their God, and they are His people, and ultimately God will share His wife's affections with no other man. The resolution of this conflict will not be the final destruction of the wife but rather her self-loathing and repentance, which brings the Savior's forgiveness and a beautiful and glorious consummation of the pure and faithful relationship that God set out to establish from the beginning.[12]

Where is the wisdom of God in allowing the development of this relationship to progress over such a rocky road? Verse 44 reveals the answer: when things are finally set right in the age to come, Israel will have not the slightest temptation to credit herself for her well-being. All glory will belong to our all-glorious Father.

Summary

The Old Testament, then, in its development of the theme of the nations and Israel's relationship to them, reveals that the godless world in the current age is destined for destruction. Out of this godless world, God has called into being a people of His own, intending to bless them and make them a channel of blessing to the other nations so that ultimately He can redeem them, too, in the millennial age to come. God's own people, though, even in their best intentions, are overcome by the powerful urges of their flesh

---

[12] To some extent this prophecy has already been fulfilled. The Babylonian captivity seems to have largely cured Israel of her lust to imitate the nations. Ever since that time the Jews have been, overall, much more willing to be distinct from the nations in their worship, their manners, and even in their dress. However, during the time between the close of the Old Testament and the destruction of Jerusalem in AD 70, Israel tended to look upon this semblance of holiness self-righteously, and she simply substituted one form of rebellion against God for another. Thus in John 8:23, in reproof of the Pharisees (cf. v. 13), Jesus said, "Ye are of this world." In externals, the Pharisees were as unlike the nations of the world as one could imagine, but in heart they were no less hostile to God, and the full deliverance prophesied by Ezekiel still awaits fulfillment.

to pattern themselves after the surrounding pagan nations. It does not seem to matter that God clearly manifests the futility of paganism by a pattern of bringing such nations to destruction under the weight of their own sins. The urges of the flesh are not to be denied, and Israel *will* be like the nations, no matter the cost. Israel's Redeemer lets His people go that way far enough to taste the bitterness of that approach to life in His world. Yet He insists that, will as she may, Israel ultimately will *not* be like the nations, for her Deliverer *will* turn her once and for all from her sins to Himself, and then will turn the rest of the nations to Himself as well. With the hymn writer may we pray, thinking of ourselves individually along with Israel and the whole world, "And Lord haste the day!"

2

DEFINING THE WORLD, PART 2:
NEW TESTAMENT TEACHING

Now Testament revelation about the world echoes key themes from the Old Testament and also expands into new territory.

ECHOES OF OLD TESTAMENT TEACHING
Several key Old Testament emphases simply extend right into the New Testament. The futility of Gentile cultures in their ignorance of God finds expression in Jesus' teaching on materialism, for example, when He warns His disciples against anxiety over physical possessions and provisions, reminding them, "After all these things do the Gentiles seek" (Matt. 6:32; Luke 12:30). He also warns His disciples not to be power-hungry and self-aggrandizing like "the princes of the Gentiles" (Matt. 20:25a; Mark 10:42; Luke 22:25). Such teaching also continues the theme of God's commands to His people not to imitate the ways of the nations. Paul echoes the same theme in two passages. "This I say therefore, and testify in the Lord, that ye henceforth walk not as other Gentiles walk" (Eph. 4:17). And in 1 Thessalonians 4:3–5 he teaches that sanctification includes controlling one's body[1] rather than living "in the lust of concupiscence, even as the Gentiles which know not God." Peter adds an admonition of his own: "For the time already past is sufficient for you to have carried out the desire of the Gentiles, having pursued a course of sensuality, lusts, drunkenness,

---

[1] Some versions speak of acquiring a wife rather than controlling one's body, but on either interpretation of the Greek text the admonition relevant for this study is the same: "Do not be like the nations [Gentiles]."

carousing, drinking parties and abominable idolatries" (1 Pet. 4:3, NASB).

Sadly, New Testament believers, like Old Testament Israel, are capable of descending into deeper debauchery than the heathen. Thus, Paul rebukes the Corinthian church:

> It is reported commonly that there is fornication among you, and such fornication as is not so much as named among the Gentiles, that one should have his father's wife. And ye are puffed up, and have not rather mourned, that he that hath done this deed might be taken away from among you (1 Cor. 5:1–2).

The focus has shifted, perhaps, from "the nations" as national bodies to "the nations" as individual Gentiles, but the emphasis is the same as we found in the Old Testament: God's people are to partake of His holiness, not participate in Gentile carnality, and it is especially grievous when believers outdo the lost in their depravity.

The destruction of the godless nations prophesied in the Old Testament is reiterated in New Testament prophecy as well. Thus, John saw in his vision that "the cities of the nations fell" (Rev. 16:19). When Christ returns to the earth, "Out of his mouth goeth a sharp sword, that with it he should smite the nations: and he shall rule them with a rod of iron: and he treadeth the winepress of the fierceness and wrath of Almighty God" (Rev. 19:15). A few verses later (Rev. 20:3), we also learn something that the Old Testament never explicitly declared about the nations: at the root of their rebellion against God lies satanic deception. It is no wonder that those who have loved Satan's lies and delighted in his charms will suffer his destiny as well.

On the bright side, however, the New Testament also pushes toward its fulfillment the Old Testament promise that Abraham's blessing would extend to all the families of the earth. The Gospel writers call attention to the benefits of Jesus' ministry for Gentiles as well as Jews. Luke, for instance, records that Simeon saw in the infant Jesus "a light to lighten the Gentiles" (Luke 2:32). Matthew explains that Joseph's selection of Nazareth as his family's home fulfilled a prophecy that Gentiles sitting in darkness would see great light (Matt. 4:15–16). Jesus commands His disciples to "teach all nations" (Matt. 28:19; Luke 24:47), and He prophesies, in words loosely echoing Israel's Old Testament assignment, that in fact "this gospel of the kingdom shall be preached in all the world for a witness unto all nations" before the end of the age (Matt. 24:14; Mark 13:10).

The ministry of Paul provides major development of this Old Testament theme, as Paul gives himself unstintingly to his service as the apostle to the Gentiles (Rom. 11:13; Gal. 2:8; 1 Tim. 2:7; 2 Tim. 1:11). This topic is worthy of extended development, but the fact that it is tangential to the focus of this book allows only the most basic description here. Paul calls attention to God's intent to extend Abraham's blessing to the whole world and to make Abraham the father of many nations, not just one or a handful (Rom. 4:17f.; Gal. 3:8, 14). He bookends his great treatise on the gospel, Romans, with references to God's intention to use evangelistic proclamation to bring all nations under Christ's lordship (Rom. 1:5; 15:8–16). In explaining the problem of Israel's rejecting her Messiah in chapters 9–11, Paul teaches that this historical development is part of God's all-wise plan. Israel's unbelief provides occasion for the gospel to go to the Gentiles. Their acceptance of it only hardens Israel in her jealousy as her own God lavishes His blessings on those whom she has always viewed, in spite of so much contrary Old Testament revelation, as outsiders to His benevolent plans. Thus, when all is said and done for eternity, both major segments of humanity will have experienced a phase of unbelief and a phase of faith, and the only explanation for anyone's ultimate faith in God will be God's free grace and mercy (Rom. 11:11–32).

The final prophecies of Scripture regarding the nations reiterate the Old Testament promises of their ultimate salvation. Seeing the Holy City, New Jerusalem, coming down from heaven, John includes in his description, "And the nations of them which are saved shall walk in the light of it: and the kings of the earth do bring their glory and honour into it," and again, "They shall bring the glory and honour of the nations into it" (Rev. 21:24–26). Finally, when John sees the tree of life, to which God banned access in the Garden of Eden after the Fall, he sees it not as a single specimen but as a whole species, growing in the most accessible places, and he adds that "the leaves of the tree were for the healing of the nations" (Rev. 22:2). Thus in the space of just six verses near the close of Scripture, John prophesies three times that the privileges and joys of heaven will be available to the nations.

EXPANSION BEYOND OLD TESTAMENT TEACHING

But what does all this New Testament revelation about the nations have to do with "the world" in the sense that this book deals with? In the Old Testament we can see that the nations presented to Israel a strong temptation to abandon her covenant with Jehovah and embrace a worldly lifestyle. The New Testament usage of "the nations," though, simply does not reflect this theme to any significant extent. This is not to say, of course, that New Testament believers experience no similar temptation or that the New Testament does not address this issue. Instead, what we see in the New Testament is a shift of vocabulary. The pagans whose lifestyles

New Testament believers are commanded not to imitate are seldom called "the nations" now; instead they are called "the world."

Shift in Terminology

What caused this vocabulary shift from the Old Testament's "the nations" to the New Testament's "the world"? Although the New Testament does not explain this shift explicitly, the reason for it seems easy enough to infer. In the Old Testament, the boundary between God's people and the lost world was, at least dominantly, a matter of national identity. Israel was God's chosen nation; the other nations remained outsiders to the main flow of His saving work in that age. This is not to say, of course, that all Israelites were in fact regenerate people or that no Gentiles were regenerate. On the one hand, God's grace has always embraced all who sincerely seek Him; on the other, mere external membership in a body of God's people has never been enough to insure saving participation in God's covenants. Still, the basic distinction holds, as Paul reminded the Gentile believers in Ephesus:

> Wherefore remember, that ye being in time past Gentiles in the flesh, who are called Uncircumcision by that which is called the Circumcision in the flesh made by hands; that at that time ye were without Christ, being aliens from the commonwealth of Israel, and strangers from the covenants of promise, having no hope, and without God in the world (Eph. 2:11–12).

Under the New Testament economy, though, things are different. The line that separates God's people from the rest of the world is no longer a matter of national identity; the gospel of Christ is for all nations (Matt. 28:19).

This difference between the Testaments was not an easy one for the first generation of Christians to understand and accept. The first New Testament record of someone's experiencing Spirit baptism into the body of Christ without any prior acceptance of Judaism appears in Acts 10. God was about to send Peter to preach the gospel to the Gentile Cornelius and his household. We would think that Peter would have jumped at the mere suggestion of such an opportunity. But God knew otherwise, and He gave Peter a vision of a sheet being lowered from heaven by its four corners. This sheet was full of animals that were unclean under the Mosaic dietary laws and was accompanied by a voice calling Peter and instructing him to kill and eat. Peter apparently thinks his obedience to God's commands is being tested because he refuses, stating that he has never eaten anything unclean. He finds that this is not a test. The reply comes back, "What I have cleansed, don't you call unclean." We might think that one such vision would be all the correction Peter needed, but in fact it takes three cycles of the same vision even to begin to convince Peter that God was introducing a major change in His working among the peoples of the earth. Even after all this, when Peter begins to speak to the group assembled at Cornelius's home, his terse introduction manifests a degree of confusion: "Ye know how that it is an unlawful thing for a man that is a Jew to keep company, or come unto one of another nation; but God hath shewed me that I should not call any man common or unclean" (Acts 10:28). The last clause shows understanding, but the first clause mistakenly[2] declares, in the present

---

[2] I say "mistakenly" on the assumption that Peter means to say that God forbids it. Some interpreters believe it is very important not to fault the behavior of the apostles, given Jesus' promises to them of special divine protection and enabling. It would be possible to maintain the correctness of Peter's statement if we assume that he refers not to what God presently forbids but to what his nation presently forbids based on God's commands in the past. I am personally inclined, especially given Paul's rebuke

tense, that Peter's presence in this gathering of Gentiles is forbidden. Clearly, Peter's conscience is not yet at ease.

When Peter later reports to his brethren that God blessed his preaching on that occasion with the same outpouring of the Holy Spirit's power as the apostles experienced at Pentecost, it is not easy for them, either, to come to terms with the full implications of what has happened. All they can say is, "Then hath God also to the Gentiles granted repentance unto life" (Acts 11:18b). The fact that the record of Acts devotes a chapter and a half to this single incident shows its importance in early church history; it is crucial for people to understand that the reason Christianity has become a largely Gentile movement is no mere sociological quirk. It is a shift that God Himself engineered, one that was not easily accomplished. This initial event did not put the matter to rest, for one of the major controversies that plagued the first generation of Christians was the question of whether faith in Christ required circumcision and adherence to the law of Moses. Put more simply, it was the question of whether a Gentile could become a Christian without first, or at least simultaneously, becoming a proselyte to Judaism.

When Paul and Barnabas returned to Antioch from their first missionary journey, one of the key points of their report was how God "had opened the door of faith unto the Gentiles" (Acts 14:27). Mass conversion of the Gentiles was not something Paul had set out to accomplish. He did not ignore the Jews in the cities where he preached; in fact, he always began at the synagogue, and his first desire was to see his countrymen embrace their Messiah. A

---

of Peter in Galatians 2:11ff., to refrain from attributing total infallibility and inerrancy to words or deeds of the apostles beyond their writing of the inspired literature.

pattern that appears in many passages in Acts is detailed early in Paul's first journey:

> And when the Jews were gone out of the synagogue, the Gentiles besought that these words might be preached to them the next sabbath. Now when the congregation was broken up, many of the Jews and religious proselytes followed Paul and Barnabas: who, speaking to them, persuaded them to continue in the grace of God. And the next sabbath day came almost the whole city together to hear the word of God. But when the Jews saw the multitudes, they were filled with envy, and spake against those things which were spoken by Paul, contradicting and blaspheming. Then Paul and Barnabas waxed bold, and said, It was necessary that the word of God should first have been spoken to you: but seeing ye put it from you, and judge yourselves unworthy of everlasting life, lo, we turn to the Gentiles. For so hath the Lord commanded us, saying, I have set thee to be a light of the Gentiles, that thou shouldest be for salvation unto the ends of the earth. And when the Gentiles heard this, they were glad, and glorified the word of the Lord: and as many as were ordained to eternal life believed (Acts 13:42–48).

Again, then, what is happening is not a matter of Paul's presenting the gospel in a manipulative way that engineers Jewish rejection and Gentile embrace, as though he had chosen to make a name for himself as the apostle to the Gentiles. Rather, the gospel is going "to the Jew first, and also to the Greek" (Rom. 1:16*b*), but in the wisdom and providence of God what eventuates is Gentile acceptance and Jewish hostility.

Even this missionary experience, however, does not settle the matter in the minds of the original Jewish Christians, and Luke records in detail the council at Jerusalem, which considered the controversy and issued a ruling (Acts 15:1–31). Beyond these portions of Acts, the epistle to the Galatians focuses on the question of whether works of law are necessary for salvation, and a significant factor in the discussion is the implication of this question for Gentile believers. The difficulty of the matter is especially apparent from the fact that even the apostolic company did not find it easy to resolve. Peter himself fell victim to the pressure of Jewish exclusivists, along with Paul's own companion Barnabas:

> But when Peter was come to Antioch, I withstood him to the face, because he was to be blamed. For before that certain came from James, he did eat with the Gentiles: but when they were come, he withdrew and separated himself, fearing them which were of the circumcision. And the other Jews dissembled likewise with him; insomuch that Barnabas also was carried away with their dissimulation. But when I saw that they walked not uprightly according to the truth of the gospel, I said unto Peter before them all, If thou, being a Jew, livest after the manner of Gentiles, and not as do the Jews, why compellest thou the Gentiles to live as do the Jews? We who are Jews by nature, and not sinners of the Gentiles, knowing that a man is not justified by the works of the law, but by the faith of Jesus Christ, even we have believed in Jesus Christ, that we might be justified by the faith of Christ, and not by the works of the law: for by the works of the law shall no flesh be justified (Gal. 2:11–16).

Finally, though, God had His way in the minds of the early church, and the Gentiles were welcomed in, and, as we know, they quickly came even to predominate, as the Jews continued to rebel and reject. Thus Peter is eventually able to write, with all sincerity, that God judges "without respect of persons" (1 Pet. 1:17), and in a particularly remarkable passage he applies to Gentile believers some of the Old Testament texts that most intimately describe God's relationship with Israel:

> But ye are a chosen generation, a royal priesthood, an holy nation, a peculiar people; that ye should shew forth the praises of him who hath called you out of darkness into his marvellous light: which in time past were not a people, but are now the people of God: which had not obtained mercy, but now have obtained mercy (1 Pet. 2:9–10).[3]

That Peter could speak to Gentiles with such warmth, in words that God so obviously intended to win and hold Jewish hearts, shows that his initial grudging acceptance of Gentile believers eventually blossomed into a heartfelt embrace.

---

[3] The Old Testament allusions are rich. Verse 9 alludes to Exodus 19:5–6: "Ye shall be a peculiar treasure unto me above all people . . . and ye shall be unto me a kingdom of priests, and an holy nation." The verse also seems to allude to Deuteronomy 4:6–8: "Keep therefore and do them; for this is your wisdom and your understanding in the sight of the nations, which shall hear all these statutes, and say, Surely this great nation is a wise and understanding people. For what nation is there so great, who hath God so nigh unto them, as the Lord our God is in all things that we call upon him for? And what nation is there so great, that hath statutes and judgments so righteous as all this law, which I set before you this day?" Verse 10 alludes to Hosea 1:6–10, referring to Hosea's children: "And she conceived again, and bare a daughter. And God said unto him, Call her name Loruhamah: for I will no more have mercy upon the house of Israel; but I will utterly take them away. . . . Now when she had weaned Loruhamah, she conceived, and bare a son. Then said God, Call his name Loammi: for ye are not my people, and I will not be your God. Yet . . . it shall come to pass, that in the place where it was said unto them, Ye are not my people, there it shall be said unto them, Ye are the sons of the living God."

Obviously, then, "the nations" is no longer appropriate as the primary expression referring to the ungodly in general. By the close of the apostolic age, the Gentiles had come to comprise the dominant part of the church. To continue using "the nations" as an expression for "the godless" would not only be confusing and even misleading at a time when national distinctions had disappeared in God's program of salvation;[4] it would also demean and discourage non-Jews who had come to rejoice in their new awareness of God's love for them. The new expressions that present themselves as more serviceable are *kosmos* ("the world") and *aion* ("the age").[5]

Usage of *Kosmos* and *Aion*

The history of the usage of these Greek words is challenging to master, as is the range of meaning they convey in the New Testament. Bauer, Danker, Arndt, and Gingrich (BDAG), the standard scholarly lexicon of the Greek New Testament in English, lists the following senses of *kosmos*:

1. that which serves to beautify through decoration, *adornment, adorning*
2. condition of orderliness, *orderly arrangement, order*[6]
3. the sum total of everything here and now, *the world, the (orderly) universe*
4. the sum total of all beings above the level of the animals, *the world*
5. planet earth as a place of inhabitation, *the world*
6. humanity in general, *the world*
7. the system of human existence in its many aspects, *the world*
8. collective aspect of an entity, *totality, sum total*[7]

---

[4] This is evident in the wording of the Great Commission.

[5] κόσμος and αἰών in Greek. *Aion* (pronounced "I own"), sometimes transliterated into English as *aeon*, is the source of our English word *eon*.

[6] This sense does not occur in the New Testament.

[7] *A Greek-English Lexicon of the New Testament and Other Early Christian Literature*, 3rd edition (BDAG), rev. and ed. by Frederick William Danker, based on Walter

Notice how many different senses of the word can be translated *world*; checking an English dictionary will confirm that the English word does have this range of meaning and can carry other senses as well.[8] It is no small task, then, to categorize the New Testament occurrences of the word and discern the precise meaning in each passage.

Aion is less complex but not without challenges. BDAG's definition includes four senses:

1. a long period of time, without reference to beginning or end, *the past, earliest times, eternity*
2. a segment of time as a particular unit of history, *age*[9]
3. the world as a spatial concept, *the world*
4. the Aeon as a person, the *Aeon*[10]

The only sense of *aion* relevant to this book is the third, where it is a very close synonym of *kosmos*.

When they refer to the physical creation, *kosmos* and *aion* do not connote moral evil. God created the world very good, and nowhere does Scripture indicate that the fall of man reversed that essential goodness. The Fall affected the whole creation negatively (Rom. 8:19–22), but, for example, matter itself did not become inherently

---

Bauer's *Griechisch-deutsches Wörterbuch zu den Schriften des Neuen Testaments und der frühchristlichen Literatur*, 6th edition, ed. Kurt Aland and Barbara Aland, with Viktor Reichmann and on previous English editions by W. F. Arndt, F. W. Gingrich, and F. W. Danker (Chicago: University of Chicago Press, 2000), 561ff.

[8] *Merriam Webster's Collegiate Dictionary*, for example, defines fourteen senses of *world*.

[9] The supporting development for this sense makes clear that the reference is to a long segment of time; the two ages named in the New Testament are "this age" and "the age to come." So this is not a word that would refer to shorter periods such as "the modern age" or "the Middle Ages." Words used for an intermediate-length period of time include καιρός (*kairos*, "time") and γενεά (*genea*, "generation"), especially in the plural.

[10] BDAG, 32ff. Most conservative interpreters reject the fourth sense for the New Testament literature.

evil because of man's sin. So these words in reference to the whole sphere of physical existence can be understood as carrying no implications about morality, or at least no implication of immorality.

This morally unspecified sense—or perhaps even morally positive sense—"the universe" certainly appears in the New Testament. Several passages, for example, refer to the beginning of time as "the foundation of the world" (e.g., Matt. 25:34; John 17:24; Eph. 1:4). Similarly Paul's sermon on Mars Hill introduces his Athenian audience to "God that made the world and all things therein" (Acts 17:24), and Hebrews refers to God as the Creator of "the worlds" (*aion*, 1:2; 11:3). But this sense is not the one that primarily concerns us.

Our study concerns itself rather with the many occurrences of *kosmos* and *aion* that include a moral stigma. In these passages the reference narrows from the whole created order to the specifically human realm in its sinfulness. Thus, again in John's Gospel, our Lord declares to His disciples, "The world cannot hate you; but me it hateth, because I testify of it, that the works thereof are evil" (John 7:7). The world is not impersonal in this passage. It produces works, and those works are immoral in quality. The reference is clearly to the mass of unregenerate humanity in its hostility toward God. Similarly, James challenges his readers: "Ye adulterers and adulteresses, know ye not that the friendship of the world is enmity with God? whosoever therefore will be a friend of the world is the enemy of God" (James 4:4). Again, "the world" in this sense is not impersonal: it is capable of friendship and enmity, and its posture toward God is hostile.

It is important to point out, in passing, that the world's hostility toward God is not always overt. The rabid belligerence, for example, of British atheist Richard Dawkins,[11] though on the rise, remains relatively uncommon. More numerous, but no less hostile in fact, are those who simply ignore God or who pattern Him after their own fancies (Ps. 50:21–22). Any failure to glorify Him as He is amounts to disloyalty and hostility.

The question arises, as we return to our word study, whether *kosmos* and *aion* are exact synonyms. The entries from the BDAG lexicon cited above show clearly that the two words cover different ranges of meaning. Thus *aion* never signifies the mass of humanity, and *kosmos* never means an extremely long period of time. When the words are used with reference to unregenerate humanity in its rejection of God, though, very little difference of meaning is apparent. *Kosmos* is more likely to be used when the focus is on geography or humanity; *aion* is more likely to be used when the focus is on the present period of time. Numerous passages show no distinct focus on one of these aspects over the others, and in such passages the words appear to be interchangeable.[12]

Kosmos and *Aion* Used with Moral Stigma

We turn our focus now to the passages where *kosmos* and *aion* are used with moral stigma, referring to humanity in its hostility toward God and to the scheme of human existence that manifests

---

[11] Richard Dawkins, *The God Delusion* (Boston: Houghton Mifflin, 2006). As another example of such belligerence, an Asian friend of mine, angry at the influence of Western culture on his country traceable to the arrival of Christian missionaries, told me what he would say if he ever met Jesus personally: "I would spit in his face."

[12] I do not mean to imply that every author does in fact interchange these words. It is noteworthy that most of the New Testament usage of *kosmos* is in John's writings (105 out of 186 occurrences), and John never uses *aion* in a sense synonymous with *kosmos*. His use of *aion* refers only to limitless time. So the student who would attempt a complete explanation of the variation between these two words would have to take into account the stylistic preferences of individual authors, which are notoriously difficult to quantify and explain, especially given the limited data available for most NT authors.

this rebellion. It is important to observe at the outset that we must be careful not to broaden the reference of these words so that we impose the Bible's negativism toward the world upon elements of human existence that the Bible does not condemn. Human rebellion ought not to exist; it does not follow, of course, that humanity ought not to exist. Certain aspects of the present, fallen scheme of human existence ought not to exist; it does not follow that there is no valid root for these things that is itself good and legitimate. For instance, the self-gratification of gluttony or sexual promiscuity ought not to exist, but food and sex are themselves good gifts of a gracious God to be enjoyed gratefully within the limits He has set for them. No one ought to seek to exalt himself in self-gratifying control over another, especially to the other's disadvantage, but the urge toward dominion reflects God's intent for man and is therefore a good whose appropriate expression is to be cultivated. The world as God created it was good, and its goodness has not been totally lost in sinful man's corruption of it. Where to draw the lines beyond which our pursuit of the good things in our Father's world becomes corrupted by worldliness will receive attention later; here I simply express the caution to help us avoid the trap of over-application in the early phase of this portion of our study.

As we begin to consider what the New Testament teaches about the fallen world, let us remind ourselves what we learned in the Old Testament about "the nations" in their rebellion against God. The nations originated in the rebellion of humanity against God at Babel in Genesis 11. As their history unfolded, they developed and engaged in all kinds of behaviors that our Father calls "abominations," the strongest possible word to indicate how intensely He detested their ways. The nations are therefore destined for destruction, unless they repent and return to the Lord.

Out of the nations, our Father called into existence a single nation through whom He determined to bless the whole world by setting into motion a plan of salvation for all who would trust in the Savior. That nation, Israel, would fulfill its destiny in part by refusing to imitate the pagan nations around her, displaying instead unqualified obedience to God's holy and righteous Law. Israel, though, proved neither able nor willing to render such obedience, and instead she developed an insatiable appetite for the ways of the nations and even for the worship of their idols. This appetite was irrational, given Israel's full knowledge that the abominations of the nations were the very reason God had destroyed the Canaanites at the time of her conquest of the Promised Land. But Israel's lust was as irresistible as it was irrational, and down the worldly way she went.

Nevertheless, Israel's Deliverer declared through the prophecy of Ezekiel that her desire to be like the nations simply would not come to pass; instead, He would deliver her from the nations and their abominable ways, and in repentance she would loathe herself for her sins. That deliverance, though accomplished to a certain extent in Israel's new willingness to be unlike the nations after the Babylonian captivity, remains to be completed, and in the meantime Israel has paid a nearly unbearable price for her worldly ways.

The New Testament's teaching on the world and on the relationship of God's people to it is strikingly similar to the Old Testament's teaching on the nations and Israel's relationship to them. Let us first give attention to New Testament detail on just what the world is, since it is no longer simply the nations other than Israel.

Nowhere does the New Testament offer an inspired definition of "the world," so we must apply ourselves to the passages where the key words appear, inferring from them what we can about the characteristics of this entity. We have seen earlier that *kosmos* and *aion* in passages that carry moral stigma are not clearly distinguishable, so for the most part we will simply consider them synonymous, referring to a combination of persons, place, and time.[13] In its broadest outline, the world in the sense that concerns us is *the totality of unregenerate persons living on the earth within some period of time, along with the habitual patterns of thought and behavior by which they express their ignorance of and insubordination to God.* What characteristics of these people, their thoughts, and their behavior does the New Testament revelation identify?

The World Is Evil

The fundamentally evil nature of the world is apparent from the kinds of actions and attitudes the New Testament writers attribute to it. Several passages call the world evil. Thus Paul reminds the Galatians of their deliverance from "this present evil world" (Gal. 1:4), and Jesus testified that the world's works are evil (John 7:7). Our Savior seems to identify the world's primary sin as unbelief when He promises that the Holy Spirit will come and convict the world "of sin, because they believe not on [Him]" (John 16:9). Paul calls the people of the world "the children of disobedience" (Eph. 2:2).[14] The wording is, more literally, "the sons of disobe-

---

[13] We have observed previously that the more clearly the context focuses on time, the more likely the word will be *aion*; the more clearly it focuses on persons or place, the more likely the word will be *kosmos*. We can add here that a focus on attitudes or behavior could go either way: *people* behave on this earth as a *place*, justifying *kosmos*, but unregenerate humanity has also displayed consistent patterns of thought and behavior over the period of its existence, justifying *aion*. I do not believe it is necessary or even helpful to insist on assigning to each occurrence of these words their respective narrow senses.

[14] Earlier in the same verse Paul speaks of his readers' having lived, prior to their salvation, "according to the course of this world." The underlying Greek phrase is significant for our study in that it combines *aion* and *kosmos* in a way unique in the New Testament, reading "the age of this world." This is perhaps the key passage that under-

dience," reflecting the same Hebrew idiom Jesus used when He nicknamed James and John the "Sons of Thunder." It is a way of referring to a person's most deeply rooted habits and instincts.[15] Just as James and John were apparently by nature boisterous and forceful, people of the world are by nature disobedient.

Certainly we need not look beyond the walls of our fundamentalist families, churches, and schools to find that same spirit—we all feel it powerfully even within ourselves. A spiritual authority who expresses an expectation for some specific form of good conduct or adherence to some biblical command can expect many under his care simply to disregard that expectation. Then, if he confronts their failure, he can expect them to retort in terms indicating neither a desire to obey nor a recognition of any valid claim on their obedience. Such attitudes reflect, at best, a capitulation to our fleshly propensity to imitate the sons of disobedience as Israel imitated the nations, and very possibly they reflect an unregenerate heart.

The World Hates Christ and Christians

Returning to our exposition of the character of the world, we learn that the world hates our Savior, precisely because He spoke out against its sinfulness. "The world cannot hate you; but me it

---

lies BDAG's fourth sense of *aion*, "the Aeon as a person." Support for that idea comes from the next phrase in the verse, "the prince of the power of the air," followed in turn by another reference to a person, "the spirit that now works in the children of disobedience." It is perhaps more likely, though, that Paul simply pairs up these two words for stylistic purposes, as he does with other pairs of words in Ephesians: words for God's will (1:5, 11), spiritual perception (1:18), power (1:19; 3:7; 6:10), law (2:15), ministry activity (4:12), full growth (4:13), deception (4:14) and the inner man (4:22). With this interpretation, the verse supports (but does not prove) the idea that *kosmos* and *aion* can sometimes be essentially synonymous.

[15] The idiom can also refer to one's destiny. Judas was the "son of perdition," and in this same passage Paul calls the unregenerate "children of wrath" (Eph. 2:3). Context decides the meaning in each case.

hateth, because I testify of it, that the works thereof are evil" (John 7:7). Later Jesus explained to the disciples that the world *would* hate them, not for their own sake, but because of their relationship with Him:

> If the world hate you, ye know that it hated me before it hated you. If ye were of the world, the world would love his own: but because ye are not of the world, but I have chosen you out of the world, therefore the world hateth you (John 15:18–19).

In His high-priestly prayer for the disciples, and by extension for us, our Lord reiterated the same idea in different words: "I have given them thy word; and the world hath hated them, because they are not of the world, even as I am not of the world" (John 17:14). We are not of the world (John 17:14) because our Savior has chosen us out of the world (John 15:19), and God gave us to Him out of the world (John 17:6). The world does not take such defection lightly. In response, it pours out its hatred. James perhaps had this teaching of Jesus in mind when he challenged his readers so strongly: "Ye adulterers and adulteresses, know ye not that the friendship of the world is enmity with God? whosoever therefore will be a friend of the world is the enemy of God" (James 4:4). Not only is siding with the world irrational for believers since the world hates our heavenly Father; it constitutes spiritual adultery, as the Old Testament so clearly and repeatedly and forcefully declares.[16] That professing believers guilty of such sin would deny

---

[16] Those wishing to search out this Old Testament theme would do well to begin in Ezekiel 16 and follow cross references from there. Of seventy verses in the King James Version Old Testament containing words with the root *harlot, adultery,* and *fornication,* I find forty that refer to Israel's spiritual adultery. For an in-depth study on the topic, see Raymond C. Ortlund, *God's Unfaithful Wife: A Biblical Theology of Spiritual Adultery* (Downers Grove, IL: InterVarsity, 2002).

its sinfulness comes as no surprise, for Proverbs 30:20 says, "Such is the way of an adulterous woman; she eateth, and wipeth her mouth, and saith, I have done no wickedness."

The world's hatred of Christ's disciples is not always overt and militant. Our adversary is highly resourceful. During Israel's time in the wilderness, Balak, the king of Moab, sought the destruction of God's people. Knowing that he lacked the military strength to overcome them, Balak attempted to hire the prophet Balaam to curse Israel. The story is familiar: every time Balaam opened his mouth, the words that emerged were God's blessing upon Israel (Num. 22–24). In Numbers 25, though, we find Moab and Midian uniting in a scheme that brought Israel under judgment by friendly overtures alluring her into idolatry and immorality. Later we find explicitly stated what we might have surmised: the scheme was Balaam's advice (Num. 31:16).

Though Balaam was executed in Israel's eventual conquest of Midian (Num. 31:8), his spirit and counsel were alive and well in the first century (Rev. 2:14) and remain with us today. *Rapture Ready! Adventures in the Parallel Universe of Christian Pop Culture* by journalist Daniel Radosh provides a close modern parallel. In the process of surveying the various expressions of popular culture to be found within American Evangelicalism, Radosh expresses disdain for the gospel and biblical morality, but he also finds strains of so-called Evangelicalism that are more congenial to his humanistic perspective on culture, politics, and morality. Radosh concludes that the best route to overcoming Fundamentalism is for moderate Christians to become assimilated into mainstream pop culture, and he calls upon secularists to build bridges and encourage such crossover. The resulting cultural ferment, he hopes, will attract even some conservatives and will curtail the influence of any remaining Fundamentalists.[17]

The World Is Morally Repulsive

A further characteristic of the world is that it is dirty and defiling. Looking to James again, we find that "pure religion and undefiled before God and the Father is this, . . . to keep [oneself] unspotted from the world" (James 1:27). The implication is that contact with the world marks one with an ugly blemish. In connection with the words "pure" and "undefiled" in the first portion of the verse, it is clear that blemishes resulting from contact with the world mark one as impure or unclean—unfit for intimacy and unhealthy to associate with. Peter speaks of those who by means of some knowledge about Christ[18] "have escaped the pollutions of the world" (2 Pet. 2:20). The Greek word[19] behind "pollutions" signifies a moral defilement resulting from the commission of some evil deed,[20] not the sort of filth that can easily be cleansed. Earlier in the same epistle, Peter speaks of "the corruption that is in the world through lust" (2 Pet. 1:4). The English text sounds like another reference to defilement, but the Greek word[21] signifies something even worse. It is corruption in the sense of organic decay,[22] such as the decomposition of a dead body, though of course Peter is speaking figuratively, in the moral realm. If a dirty body is

---

[17] Daniel Radosh, *Rapture Ready! Adventures in the Parallel Universe of Christian Pop Culture* (New York: Scribner, 2008), 303ff. I recommend this book only for the purpose of a mature believer's gaining insight into how evangelical Christianity is perceived by a thoughtful and articulate secular humanist and for taking warning regarding important cultural trends. The language is occasionally profane or obscene, and Radosh's skillful wit and reasoning make him effective in Satan's service.

[18] Within the larger context it appears that those to whom Peter refers never came to a saving knowledge of Christ.

[19] μίασμα (*miasma*).

[20] BDAG, 650.

[21] φθορά (*phthora*).

[22] Ibid., 1054f.

objectionable, what is a rotting one? To our Father's pure eyes, this present evil world is utterly repulsive.

The World Is Self-Focused

Of course one of the best-known passages describing the character of the world is 1 John 2:16: "For all that is in the world, the lust of the flesh, and the lust of the eyes, and the pride of life, is not of the Father, but is of the world." This listing of three elements of the world is often understood as providing a categorization of worldly things (cf. v. 15, "the things that are in the world"). The idea seems attractive with respect to some of the worldly preoccupations that first come to mind. Bodily pleasures go naturally with "lust of the flesh," and the acquisitive impulse corresponds easily to "lust of the eyes." "The pride of life" sounds like it might encompass various forms of worldly status. Many worldly interests, though, would be difficult to categorize. Take for example, someone with a worldly passion for an in-ground swimming pool.[23] This passion would be the lust of the flesh insofar as the person's desire was for bodily pleasure, the lust of the eyes insofar as it was for the pool's beauty, and the pride of life insofar as it was for the status and popularity the pool would bring.

A better approach, I believe, grows out of noticing the nature of the key words in each phrase: *lust* and *pride* name not the kinds of worldly things we might set our hearts on, but rather the aspects of fallen human nature that worldly things appeal to. Any given worldly object may appeal to any combination of these fallen pre-dispositions. In its sinfulness and enmity toward God, the world pursues bodily pleasure, visual gratification, and the boastful

---

[23] I do not mean to imply that in-ground swimming pools are inherently worldly; only that a passion to own one may well be so.

self-congratulation that accompanies wealth and status.[24] Of course, John's use of such negatively charged words as *lust*, *flesh*, and *pride* makes clear that he is not speaking of a proper appreciation for and use of God's provisions, for His glory, but rather an inordinate pursuit of such things for the sake of gratifying or exalting oneself.

Careful consideration of Titus 2:12 brings to light an interesting contrast between the world and healthy Christian character. In setting forth the characteristics of a grace-taught life, Paul calls for living "soberly, righteously, and godly in this present world" (*aion*). The Greek word translated "soberly" probably indicates self-control, a major emphasis in Titus (1:8; 2:2, 4, 5, 6, 12), set forth to correct the Cretans' self-indulgent character as lazy gluttons (1:12). Self-controlled living will require "denying ungodliness and worldly (*kosmikos*, related to *kosmos*) lusts. Paul's word "denying" implies that the world's mode of living is the opposite of self-controlled: the world is unrestrained in pursuit of its passions.

The Root of the World's Evil Character
At the bottom of the world's evil character lies this simple but far-reaching failure: the world does not know God. The passage we have just been considering implies this fact by drawing such a sharp distinction between God and the world:

> If any man love the world, the love of the Father is not in him. For all that is in the world, the lust of the flesh, and the lust of the eyes, and the pride of life, is not of the Father, but is of the world (1 John 2:15b–16).

Other passages state explicitly that the world does not know God. Just a few verses later in the same epistle, John writes, "The world

---

[24] The ideas of boastful self-congratulation and wealth or status reflect the meanings of the underlying Greek words.

knoweth us not, because it knew him not" (1 John 3:1*b*). This echoes the teaching of John's Gospel, "He was in the world, and the world was made by him, and the world knew him not" (John 1:10). Paul declares, "The world . . . knew not God" (1 Cor. 1:21) and, using the Old Testament expression, refers to "the Gentiles which know not God" (1 Thess. 4:5).

Returning to John's first epistle, we find that the world not only does not know God in Christ; it apparently asserts itself to prevent others from knowing Him as well. This is the implication of the way John combines the ideas of knowing God and overcoming the world. Just prior to his warning against loving the world, John addresses three groups within his readership as follows:

> I write unto you, little children, because your sins are forgiven you for his name's sake. I write unto you, fathers, because ye have known him that is from the beginning. I write unto you, young men, because ye have overcome the wicked one. I write unto you, little children, because ye have known the Father. I have written unto you, fathers, because ye have known him that is from the beginning. I have written unto you, young men, because ye are strong, and the word of God abideth in you, and ye have overcome the wicked one (1 John 2:12–14).

Three times in this passage John refers to knowing God, and twice to overcoming the world. Apparently these two things are connected. In chapter 5 he makes the connection more explicit:

> For whatsoever is born of God overcometh the world: and this is the victory that overcometh the world, even our faith. Who is he that overcometh the world, but he that believeth that Jesus is the Son of God? (1 John 5:4–5).

He does not use the exact phrase "know God" here, but surely being born of God and believing in Jesus as God's Son are practically equivalent to knowing God. To come into such a relationship with God, John declares, is tantamount to overcoming the world. One of the most important facts that anyone wishing to identify and relate scripturally to the world must keep always in mind is this: the world is aggressively and intransigently opposed to the knowledge of God. This opposition is perhaps one reason that our Father promised so often through Ezekiel that, after some prominent, large-scale action asserting His sovereignty over the world's affairs, "They shall know that I am the Lord."[25]

Just as the world does not know God, neither does it know God's children. "Behold, what manner of love the Father hath bestowed upon us, that we should be called the sons of God: therefore the world knoweth us not, because it knew him not" (1 John 3:1). The world does recognize its own kind, however. After saying, "Many false prophets are gone out into the world" (1 John 4:1*b*), John eventually adds,

> They are of the world: therefore speak they of the world, and the world heareth them. We are of God: he that knoweth God heareth us; he that is not of God heareth not us. Hereby know we the spirit of truth, and the spirit of error (1 John 4:5–6).

A believer whose life truly testifies of God has no reason to expect worldly people to appreciate or understand him, except for those whose hearts our Father is drawing to the Savior. Again, John speaks in terms of two mutually exclusive categories. On the one side are those who are "of the world" (v. 5); these are "not of God"

---

[25] I find expressions of this sort occurring at least 55 times in Ezekiel.

(v. 6). On the other are those who are "of God"; this category is essentially synonymous with knowing God (v. 6). These two categories are fundamentally and irreconcilably opposed to one another. A person belongs to one or the other; belonging to both is impossible.

Is there no such thing, then, as a worldly Christian? That conclusion does not follow, for we have seen that the Scripture testifies repeatedly to the fact that God's people, though they are not the world, nevertheless are very prone to imitate the world. Hardly a more pitiful condition can be imagined, as though a wealthy farmer's children would want to eat slop and wallow with the hogs. A good medicine for this condition is a prolonged meditation on our Savior's high-priestly prayer for us in John 17, which will receive attention later.

The World, the Flesh and the Devil

A crucial question arises at this point. Where does the world get its power? What persuasion could make humans clamor for mud and hog slop? Such a clamor is unthinkable, and yet every believer every day feels the almost gravitational pull of the world's attractions on his heart, even while his head tells him that these things are the moral equivalent of the pigpen. A man, for example, comes across a magazine advertisement featuring an alluring model. The advertised product itself may not even catch his notice, and if it does, the ad may produce no desire for it. But something in that advertisement does incline him to pause, perhaps for a long time, before turning the page. What is the power behind that attraction? A woman may see a similar page with a male model advertising a box of chocolates. Perhaps she doesn't even notice the man, but she may pause just as long over the chocolate as her husband or brother does over the woman. If she is dieting, her brain may tell her that the chocolate is her enemy, not her friend, yet all of her impeccable reasoning will not quench her longing for it. Where does this power lie?

The Bible is not silent on this topic. The power of the world lies in the combination of Satan's activity in opposition to God and the sinful nature of fallen human flesh. Jesus spoke three times in John's Gospel of "the prince of this world" (12:31; 14:30; 16:11). In none of these passages does He add any information about what this person does; He simply asserts his existence, notes that He and this prince have nothing in common, and announces this prince's judgment.

Paul goes further, saying in 1 Corinthians 2:12 that "we have received, not the spirit of the world, but the spirit which is of God; that we might know the things that are freely given to us of God." Given the contrast between "the spirit of the world" and "the spirit which is of God," it seems that Paul is here referring to a person who animates the world system, and again we see that the world's activity stands in conflict with our spiritual knowledge. Paul gives a little more detail yet in 2 Corinthians 4:4, where he writes regarding lost people that "the god of this world hath blinded the minds of them which believe not, lest the light of the glorious gospel of Christ, who is the image of God, should shine unto them." Here we see that this person imposes on the unregenerate mind a blindness preventing such a mind from recognizing spiritual truth. Is there any reason not to believe that he works similarly to blind the minds of believers, trying to confuse us about the difference between hog slop and heavenly treasure? Yes, a great deal of the forcefulness with which the world asserts itself is due to the supernatural power of its prince.

But Jesus stands as the example of a man who was not subject to that power (John 14:30). A magnet strong enough to hoist a bulldozer cannot lift a twig. Thus Jesus, lacking the sinful nature that our adversary's seductions play upon, overcame Satan's most powerful temptations by simple reliance on His Father's Word (Matt. 4:1–11; Luke 4:1–13). On fallen human nature, though, Satan exerts an attraction that is humanly irresistible. If he is a magnet, our flesh is a pile of iron filings, helpless against his drawing power. So one factor in the process of temptation and sin is the nature of our flesh. Enticed by our adversary's crafty salesmanship, all too readily we take hog slop for gold. Thus Paul explains to the Corinthians, "The natural man receiveth not the things of the Spirit of God: for they are foolishness unto him: neither can he know them, because they are spiritually discerned" (1 Cor. 2:14). To the flesh, the values of things have been inverted: spiritual truth is foolishness.

The absolute dichotomy between the divine nature and the nature of fallen human flesh appears most clearly in this extended discussion found in Romans 8:

> For what the law could not do, in that it was weak through the flesh, God sending his own Son in the likeness of sinful flesh, and for sin, condemned sin in the flesh: that the righteousness of the law might be fulfilled in us, who walk not after the flesh, but after the Spirit. For they that are after the flesh do mind the things of the flesh; but they that are after the Spirit the things of the Spirit. For to be carnally minded is death; but to be spiritually minded is life and peace. Because the carnal mind is enmity against God: for it is not subject to the law of God, neither indeed

can be. So then they that are in the flesh cannot please God (Rom. 8:3–8).

Our flesh, then, provides our adversary easy access to us, allowing him to alienate us from all that is good and allure us with all that is evil. Nor should we expect our flesh to improve as we progress in sanctification. Nowhere in Scripture do we find a hint that our flesh with its antipathy toward God and holiness ever weakens or disappears; in fact, Romans 8:7 (cited just above) explicitly states that the fleshly mind is unable to submit to God's law. Our flesh, as the word itself suggests, is integrally connected with our mortal bodies[26] and will finally be eliminated only when these bodies either die or are transformed at the Rapture. For the duration of our current existence, then, every believer must contend against a certain part of his own being that hates the heavenly Father.

This trio—the world, the flesh, and the Devil—has sometimes been called the unholy trinity that threatens the welfare of the human soul. The Bible passage that I find comes nearest to bringing these three together is James 3:15, where James calls attitudes of envy and strife "earthly, sensual, [and] devilish," in contrast to heavenly wisdom.[27] The exact phrase "the world, the flesh, and the devil," though, is not of biblical coinage. It goes back at least as far as a work, traditionally attributed to twelfth-century theologian Peter Abelard,[28] entitled *An Exposition of the Lord's Prayer*:

---

[26] I do not mean to *equate* the flesh and the body. Thinking and desiring, actions of the inner man, are also ascribed to the flesh (Rom. 8:7; Eph. 2:3).

[27] Another possible source is 1 John 2:16. "The lust of the flesh" obviously connects with the flesh; "the lust of the eyes" may connect with the world, since the eye is the primary means by which we take in our surroundings; "the pride of life" may connect with the devil, since his fall as recounted in Isaiah 14 features the proud boast, "I will be like the most High" (v. 14).

[28] A discussion of authorship, including alternative suggestions, appears in Charles S. F. Burnett, "The 'Expositio Orationis Dominicae' «Multorum Legimus Orationes»: Abelard's Exposition of the Lord's Prayer?" *Revue Bénédictine* 95 (1985), 60ff.

"There are three things that tempt us, the flesh, the world and the devil."[29] Thomas Aquinas in his thirteenth-century *Summa Theologica* wrote, "Further, just as man is tempted by the flesh, so too is he tempted by the world and the devil."[30] The Anglican *Book of Common Prayer*, at least as early as the 1662 edition, includes in its Litany the following petition or one similar: "From fornication and all other deadly sin; and from all the deceits of the world, the flesh, and the devil, Good Lord, deliver us."[31]

Though "the world, the flesh and the Devil" is not Bible language, it certainly captures well the Bible's testimony that the flesh is one's enemy within, the Devil is his enemy without, and the world is the Devil's kingdom, populated with so many zealots for his cause that resistance seems not only futile but foolish. These three reinforce one another with such effectiveness that a mere human, in himself, is utterly unable to withstand the combination of assaults and allurements with which the adversary coerces his submission.

Rescue from the World

Is it any wonder, then, that the New Testament speaks so often of the believer's *deliverance* from the world? The New Testament outlook is not so much that the world is a pleasant thing that believers are forbidden to participate in, though Hebrews 11:25

---

[29] This work does not seem to be available in English. It appears in Latin in "Peter Abaelard: Expositiones," posted at http://www.abaelard.de/abaelard/050511expositio .htm, accessed July 19, 2010. The Latin text is, "Tria autem sunt quae nos tentant, caro, mundus, diabolus."

[30] Thomas Aquinas, *Summa Theologica* Part 2, Question LV, First Article (in standard form, 2-2, 55, 1). *World, flesh,* and *devil* appear together elsewhere in his writings as well.

[31] The Litany, a series of brief prayer petitions, is described as follows: "Here followeth the Litany, or General Supplication, to be sung or said after Morning Prayer on Sundays, Wednesdays, and Fridays, and at other times when it shall be commanded by the Ordinary." See the Table of Contents of any copy of the *Book of Common Prayer* for the location of the Litany in that particular edition.

does acknowledge that sin is temporarily pleasurable. Rather, the New Testament portrays the world as an impending disaster from which our Father graciously delivers His children.

John Bunyan certainly perceived this scriptural emphasis, and in the narrative of his *Pilgrim's Progress* he portrays the world in terms of a fair, held all year long, in a town named Vanity. He describes the location of Vanity: "The way to the Celestial City lies just through this Town, where this lusty Fair is kept; and he that will go to the City, and yet not go through this Town, must needs go out of the World."[32] Christian and his companion Faithful find no welcome in Vanity Fair; indeed Faithful dies here as a martyr— what a deliverance! The portrait of the town and of its dealings with the two Christians is at once as sobering, instructive, and humorous as anything you are likely to find between the covers of a book. Bunyan's skillful portrait of Vanity Fair impresses the reader that it is indeed a place to be delivered from.[33]

But, of course, the Bible, not Bunyan, is our authority. Paul declares that our Savior "gave himself for our sins, that he might deliver us from this present evil world" (Gal. 1:4). Today's fundamentalist Christians are quite happy to think of Christ as giving Himself for our sins. Paul does not stop there, though. Have we thought much about the fact that, according to this passage, atonement for sins is a means to the further purpose of delivering us from the world?

---

[32] John Bunyan, *The Pilgrim's Progress* (Urichsville, OH: Barbour and Company, n.d.), 99. There are, of course, many editions of *The Pilgrim's Progress*, with varying pagination. This quotation appears near the beginning of the section on Vanity Fair, about halfway through Part One of the work.

[33] What would Bunyan say, then, to those of today's believers who indulgently enjoy the world-glamorizing magazine that so insolently adopts that very name?

The Greek word translated "deliver"[34] is used twice in Acts 7 for God's rescuing activity: first when He rescued Joseph from his afflictions (v. 10) and then when He rescued the whole nation from Egypt (v. 34). In Acts 23:27, Claudius Lysias, a high-ranking military officer, uses the word in his letter to the governor Felix, to describe how he rescued Paul from the hands of the Jews who were on the verge of killing him (cf. Acts 21:31). This is a word, then, that people used when they were talking about a dramatic deliverance from intense danger or affliction. Thus in Galatians 1:4 Paul implies that the world represents a grave danger to our welfare and our very life, from which Christ rescued us at the expense of *His* very life. And yet we wish to toy with the world and enjoy it, and we become resentful of spiritual authorities that forbid us its death-dealing pleasures?

The word *grace* is often bandied about in our day as though it implies a freedom from spiritual restraint. Paul entertained no such idea. In one of the New Testament's richest statements of the gospel, Paul teaches,

> For the grace of God that bringeth salvation hath appeared to all men, teaching us that, denying ungodliness and worldly lusts, we should live soberly, righteously, and godly, in this present world; looking for that blessed hope, and the glorious appearing of the great God and our Saviour Jesus Christ; who gave himself for us, that he might redeem us from all iniquity, and purify unto himself a peculiar people, zealous of good works (Titus 2:11–14).

[34] ἐξαιρέω (*exaireo*).

This sentence is worth a book of its own. Here we must content ourselves with the observation that disciplinary instruction[35] training us to deny worldly lusts is a function of God's saving *grace*. When some attraction can be discerned as manifesting the character of the world, true grace extends no smiling approval, permission, or tolerance. What grace is it that wishes a drowning child a pleasant swim? The problem, of course, is that, unlike drowning, our adversary's ways of killing us are so delightful that we fail to notice what he is doing. Because his poison-laced drinks taste so sweet, delightedly we drink on. When will we awaken to the Word of God and believe it? The world is a mortal danger from which our Savior shed His blood to deliver us and which He graciously disciplines us to shun.

Paul is not the only New Testament writer to speak in such terms. Let us examine the greeting of Peter's second epistle:

> Grace and peace be multiplied unto you through the knowledge of God, and of Jesus our Lord, according as his divine power hath given unto us all things that pertain unto life and godliness, through the knowledge of him that hath called us to glory and virtue: whereby are given unto us exceeding great and precious promises: that by these ye might be partakers of the divine nature, having escaped the corruption that is in the world through lust (2 Pet. 1:2–4).

Here again appears the idea of grace (v. 2), which comes through the knowledge of God and Christ. The multiplication of grace that Peter wishes for his readers is connected with God's having provided us everything necessary for life and godliness, again through

---

[35] This is the meaning of the Greek word παιδεύω (*paideuo*), translated "teaching."

the knowledge of God. (Recall here our earlier observation that perhaps the most fundamental problem with the world is that it does not know God.) Among the things God has given us are wonderful promises, which include our sharing in God's very nature. At this point Peter injects a complementary consideration: in order to be like God, we must be *unlike* the world. Thus part of what God has provided us is *escape* from "the corruption that is in the world through lust."

We earlier discussed the word translated "corruption"; it refers here to the moral decomposition, decay, or rot that characterizes the world. Here we can pause to note the additional factor that this moral rot is caused by, or is at least closely associated with, lust. The pursuit of a worldly desire always entails as a side effect the breakdown of something healthy and valuable. This is true in relationships. When a spouse or a parent or a child or a sibling insists on pursuing some self-gratifying desire at the expense of the other party, relational breakdown is inevitable. How many are the wealthy who lie on their deathbeds grieving that they are loved by no one? How many are the marriages and parent-child relationships that begin with delight but steadily decay into conflict and bitter tears? Of course such decay is not restricted to relationships. How many bodies, once strong and fit, either shrivel or balloon into uselessness because of some addiction to food, drink, or drug? It is no grace that smiles upon such self-destructive behavior; God's grace provides escape from such awful experience.

The Impermanence of the World
A final aspect of the New Testament's description of the world for our consideration is its transitory nature. A hint of the world's impermanence is contained in the phrase "this world," used thirty-eight times in the King James Version. The phrase implies that

there is another world, and its contexts generally suggest the inferiority of this one. Some passages, though, speak more explicitly. Paul told the Corinthians that "the fashion of this world passeth away" (1 Cor. 7:31*a*). John added, after his important admonition not to love the world, "And the world passeth away, and the lust thereof: but he that doeth the will of God abideth for ever" (1 John 2:17).

The world's eventual end will be no easy and pleasant one. Human history contains one example of this already: the world that perished in the Flood. Noah "condemned the world" (Heb. 11:7), and God "spared not the old world, . . . bringing in the flood upon the world of the ungodly" (2 Pet. 2:5). The present world is moving toward the same destiny, except that its next destruction will be by fire and will be total (2 Pet. 3:6–10). Jesus told His disciples, "Now is the judgment of this world: now shall the prince of this world be cast out" (John 12:31). We have observed already that the world is intransigent in its hostility toward God; here let us add that it cannot win. Already in His first coming, Jesus declared, "Be of good cheer; I have overcome the world" (John 16:33*b*). Paul gives a personal twist to the point; speaking of God's stern corrective dealings with us, he writes, "We are chastened of the Lord, that we should not be condemned with the world" (1 Cor. 11:32). Poor Demas, then, who abandoned the ministry out of love for the present world (2 Tim. 4:10)! If we see him in heaven, he can tell us what he had to suffer as the Good Shepherd graciously brought him home. If not, his story will pretty well tell itself.

DETAILED THEOLOGICAL DEFINITION OF "THE WORLD"

We began the New Testament section of our biblical study with the understanding that the world is, essentially, the totality of unregenerate persons living on the earth within some period of time, along with the habitual patterns of thought and behavior by which they express ignorance of and insubordination to God. Having examined the various aspects of the New Testament's teaching about the identity and character of the world, we are now in a position to construct a more detailed and precise definition. *The world is a spiritual kingdom ruled by Satan, in unremitting conflict with the kingdom of God, consisting visibly of the mass of living people who do not know God, and who, in response to satanic allurement that plays upon and preys upon fallen human nature, corrupt the various aspects of God's earthly creation into avenues for the gratification of self instead of the glory of God, thereby incurring eternal judgment and destruction.* The elements of this definition will provide biblical guidance for discerning and ultimately defeating the world.

3

DISCERNING THE WORLD, PART 1:
MATTERS DISCUSSED EXPLICITLY IN SCRIPTURE

It is time to apply the biblical teaching about the world to our lifestyle as believers. Four summary facts on which to build this application are these:

1. The world as we have defined it does exist.
2. The world is ubiquitous. It is all around us and, embodied in our fallen flesh, it is within us.
3. Our Father has graciously rescued us from the world; we no longer belong to it.
4. Our Father graciously commands us not to imitate the world or participate in its pursuits.

Paralleling the Old Testament's concern for the holiness of Israel among the nations, the New Testament also warns against worldliness. "Be not conformed to this world" (Rom. 12:2a); "Be ye not unequally yoked together with unbelievers" (2 Cor. 6:14a); "Walk not as other Gentiles walk" (Eph. 4:17b); "Love not the world" (1 John 2:15a). Clearly, believers' conduct is to differ radically from that of the unbelievers among whom they live.

We will develop this New Testament emphasis in three chapters. The present chapter will identify forms of worldliness that Scripture explicitly points out. Since the world consists of lost humanity in its rejection of and rebellion against God, this chapter could theoretically expand to include everything that the Bible calls sin. We will restrict our discussion to several key passages specifically warning believers to avoid patterns of ungodly conduct evident in the surrounding culture. Chapter Four will discuss the obligation that Scripture places upon its readers to apply its principles discerningly to matters not directly discussed. Chapter Five will consider some guidelines for applying Scripture's teaching on worldliness.[1] Throughout, some discussion of specific areas of contemporary culture appears as well.

Ephesians 4:17–5:21

The New Testament's lengthiest discussion of specific points at which believers are to behave differently from the world is in Ephesians 4:17–5:21.[2] I hesitate to take the space to print the whole passage, but it is vital that our thinking be oriented to what God Himself says. Please read the passage thoughtfully, noticing how thoroughly it reflects so much of what our study thus far has covered.

> This I say therefore, and testify in the Lord, that ye henceforth walk not as other Gentiles walk, in the vanity of their mind, having the understanding darkened, being alienated from the life of God through the ignorance that is in them, because of the blindness of their heart: who being past feeling have given themselves over unto lasciviousness, to work all uncleanness with greediness. But ye have not so learned Christ; if so be that ye have heard him, and have been taught by him, as the truth is in Jesus: that ye put off concerning the former conversation the old man, which is corrupt according to the deceitful lusts; and be

---

[1] Useful works treating the topic of Bible application include, in no particular order, William W. Klein, Craig L. Blomberg, and Robert L. Hubbard Jr., *Introduction to Biblical Interpretation*, rev. ed. (Nashville: Thomas Nelson, 2004); Daniel M. Doriani, *Putting the Truth to Work: The Theory and Practice of Biblical Application* (Phillipsburg, NJ: Presbyterian and Reformed, 2001); Roberston McQuilkin, *Understanding and Applying the Bible*, rev. ed. (Chicago: Moody, 1992); and Dave Veerman, *How to Apply the Bible* (Wheaton, IL: Tyndale, 1993).

[2] Colossians 3:1–13 is a close parallel.

renewed in the spirit of your mind; and that ye put on the new man, which after God is created in righteousness and true holiness.

Wherefore putting away lying, speak every man truth with his neighbour: for we are members one of another. Be ye angry, and sin not: let not the sun go down upon your wrath: neither give place to the devil. Let him that stole steal no more: but rather let him labour, working with his hands the thing which is good, that he may have to give to him that needeth. Let no corrupt communication proceed out of your mouth, but that which is good to the use of edifying, that it may minister grace unto the hearers. And grieve not the holy Spirit of God, whereby ye are sealed unto the day of redemption. Let all bitterness, and wrath, and anger, and clamour, and evil speaking, be put away from you, with all malice: and be ye kind one to another, tenderhearted, forgiving one another, even as God for Christ's sake hath forgiven you.

Be ye therefore followers of God, as dear children; and walk in love, as Christ also hath loved us, and hath given himself for us an offering and a sacrifice to God for a sweetsmelling savour.

But fornication, and all uncleanness, or covetousness, let it not be once named among you, as becometh saints; neither filthiness, nor foolish talking, nor jesting, which are not convenient: but rather giving of thanks. For this ye know, that no whoremonger, nor unclean person, nor covetous man, who is an idolater, hath any inheritance in the kingdom of Christ and of God. Let no man deceive you with vain words: for because of these things cometh the wrath of God upon the children of disobedience. Be not ye therefore partakers with them. For ye were sometimes darkness, but now are ye light in the Lord: walk as children of light: (for the fruit of the Spirit is in all goodness and righteousness and truth;) proving what is acceptable unto the Lord. And have no fellowship with the unfruitful works of darkness, but rather reprove them. For it is a shame even to speak of those things which are done of them in secret. But all things that are reproved are made manifest by the light: for whatsoever doth make manifest is light. Wherefore he saith, Awake thou that sleepest, and arise from the dead, and Christ shall give thee light.

See then that ye walk circumspectly, not as fools, but as wise, redeeming the time, because the days are evil. Wherefore be ye not unwise, but understanding what the will of the Lord is. And be not drunk with wine, wherein is excess; but be filled with the Spirit; speaking to yourselves in psalms and hymns and spiritual songs, singing and making melody in your heart to the Lord; giving thanks always for all things unto God and the Father in the name of our Lord Jesus Christ; submitting yourselves one to another in the fear of God.

After its opening discussion of the fundamental difference between believers and the world in terms of their relationship with God (4:17–24), the passage goes on to list at least seven sins common to the Gentiles that Christians must avoid: lying (4:25), inordinate anger (4:26, 31), stealing (4:28), evil speech (4:29, 31; 5:4), fornication (5:3), covetousness (5:3), and drunkenness (5:18).[3] Also included are a strong warning that people whose lives are characterized by these sins are excluded from God's kingdom (5:5–6), a second assertion of the fundamental difference in spiritual character between believers and the world (5:7–14), and an appeal for wisdom rather than foolishness (5:15–17). It is not, then, as though Paul kindly and unobtrusively appeals, "Let me suggest, please, some points that you might do well to consider." Rather, in strong and pointed language, Paul asserts the folly—indeed the spiritually suicidal nature—of behaving like an unbeliever. And he goes even further. It is not enough for believers merely to refrain from such behaviors; we are to assert ourselves in correcting those who behave so (5:11).

How well are we doing at obeying this passage? How long has it been since you were last lied to by a fellow believer? How long since you last lied? Most of us can probably go right down the list and name recent instances of just these behaviors within our close circle of Christian friends and family, especially when we consider that there is no reason to interpret these sins narrowly. Lying, for example, is not restricted to giving false information in face-to-face conversation. Someone who falsifies information on a tax form in order to reduce tax liability, for example, is guilty of both lying and stealing. The deeper sin of covetousness is very likely present as the motive, possibly accompanied by inordinate anger as well.

---

[3] Two other prohibitions appear, "Neither give place to the devil" (4:27) and "Grieve not the holy Spirit of God" (4:30). I did not include them in the list because they do not connect so clearly with specific worldly behaviors. If "giving place to the devil" refers to various forms of spiritism, then it would certainly deserve recognition as a separate item on the list. Much more likely, though, is that this prohibition simply expands the prohibition against anger. The Greek word for *devil* means "slanderer"; inordinate anger provides Satan an opportunity to stir up gossip and false accusations.

Guilty as we are, we tend nevertheless to condemn those who appear to us even more guilty ("At least we don't drink or fornicate—well, not much anyhow"), while letting ourselves entirely off the hook ("Yes, there are a lot of worldly Christians out there, but not me!"). This is not the thinking of those who have indeed "learned Christ" (4:20). New creatures in Christ have been created in righteousness and true holiness (4:24). Even new creatures will continue to feel the pull of the flesh back to the world, of course, but something is seriously amiss when they defend as their Christian liberty behavior that Scripture so clearly calls disobedience subject to God's wrath (5:6).

We will miss an important aspect of this passage, though, if we view it as purely negative. Of the 626 words in the passage (as rendered in the KJV), the number of words expressing a negative or disapproving tone toward people or actions is not much greater than the number expressing a positive tone (290 vs. 249 by my count). Most of the prohibitions in the passage are offset by a positive command, as shown in the table below, and the sequence of presentation puts the accent on the positive. Where there is a positive command, the value of the corresponding negative lies not so much in itself as in its necessity as prerequisite to the positive.

Reference	Sin prohibited	Virtue required
4:25	lying	speaking truth
4:26f., 31f.	inordinate anger and expressions of malice	appropriate anger (?); kindness and forgiveness
4:28	stealing	working and giving
4:29, 31; 5:4	corrupt and immoral speech	edifying speech; thanksgiving
5:3	sexual immorality	—
5:3	covetousness	—
5:18	drunkenness	Spirit filling

As we consider the teaching of this passage on the topic of worldliness, then, we must recognize that it calls upon believers not only to shun the vices that the world practices but also to practice the virtues that the world shuns. Obeying the prohibitions but not the positive commands does not constitute the true holiness in which verse 24 rejoices.

TITUS 2–3

Titus 2–3 is another passage that lists negative characteristics of the world that believers are not to display, along with positive virtues to develop. Chapter 2 divides believers into social categories for which the various items listed are especially relevant. Paul makes the connection to the world in verse 12, in a section that provides the rationale for insisting on these behaviors. Believers should live as outlined because God's saving grace teaches us, among other things, to deny "worldly lusts." Similarly, chapter 3 opens with a call for several points of Christian character and conduct, noting again that to live otherwise is to fail to emerge from our pre-conversion lifestyle (3:3ff.).

Ref.	Category Addressed	Negative	Positive
2:2	older men		sober
			grave
			temperate
			sound in faith
			sound in charity
			sound in patience
			showing all meekness to all men

Ref.	Category Addressed	Negative	Positive
2:3	older women		in behavior as becometh holiness
		not false accusers	
		not given to much wine	
			teachers of good things
2:4–5	young women		love their husbands
			love their children
			discreet
			chaste
			keepers at home
			good
			obedient to their own husbands
2:6	young men		sober minded
2:7–8	Titus (pastors)		a pattern of good works
			uncorruptness
			gravity
			sincerity
			sound speech
2:9–10	servants		obedient to their masters
			please their masters well
		not answering again (back-talking)	
		not purloining (embezzling)	
			showing all good fidelity
			showing all meekness to all men

Ref.	Category Addressed	Negative	Positive
3:1–2	all Christians		be subject to principalities and powers
			obey magistrates
			be ready to every good work
		speak evil of no man	
		be no brawlers	
			gentle
			showing all meekness to all men

The correspondence between the negative and positive categories is not as strong as in the Ephesians passage, but most of the same ideas do recur. Here the emphasis on the positive is even stronger than in Ephesians. The world will always view godly Christians through its distorted lens, so its evaluation of believers is unreliable, but the "un-worldliness" that mature Christians see in one another—and that God sees in us—ought to be, at the very least, no less a matter of the positives in which we engage than the negatives from which we abstain.

2 TIMOTHY 3:1–5

This passage paints a highly negative picture of the moral character that prevails in the last days, listing eighteen kinds of evil characterizing that generation. Most of these descriptors are a single word in Greek, rendered variously by the English versions as shown in the following table, with boldface type calling attention to the most significant differences from the KJV.

"In the last days, . . . men shall be . . ."

Verse	Greek	VERSION			
		KJV	NKJ	NASB	ESV
2	φίλαυτοι	lovers of their own selves	lovers of themselves	lovers of self	lovers of self
	φιλάργυροι	covetous	lovers of money	lovers of money	lovers of money
	ἀλαζόνες	boasters	boasters	boastful	proud
	ὑπερήφανοι	proud	proud	arrogant	arrogant
	βλάσφημοι	blasphemers	blasphemers	revilers	abusive[4]
	γονεῦσιν ἀπειθεῖς	disobedient to parents	disobedient to parents	disobedient to parents	disobedient to their parents
	ἀχάριστοι	unthankful	unthankful	ungrateful	ungrateful
	ἀνόσιοι	unholy	unholy	unholy	unholy
3	ἄστοργοι	without natural affection	unloving	unloving	heartless
	ἄσπονδοι	trucebreakers	unforgiving	irreconcilable	unappeasable
	διάβολοι	false accusers	slanderers	malicious gossips	slanderous
	ἀκρατεῖς	incontinent	without self-control	without self-control	without self-control
	ἀνήμεροι	fierce	brutal	brutal	brutal
	ἀφιλάγαθοι	despisers of those that are good	despisers of good	haters of good	not loving good
4	προδόται	traitors	traitors	treacherous	treacherous
	προπετεῖς	heady	headstrong	reckless	reckless
	τετυφωμένοι	highminded	haughty	conceited	swollen with conceit
	φιλήδονοι μᾶλλον ἢ φιλόθεοι	lovers of pleasure more than lovers of God	lovers of pleasure rather than lovers of God	lovers of pleasure rather than lovers of God	lovers of pleasure rather than lovers of God

---

[4] The rendering "abusive" is potentially misleading. The Greek word refers specifically to defamatory speech.

If you did not read the passage above carefully, I ask that you do so before continuing. I suspect that most readers at least forty years old who have not recently thought much about this passage will share the impression I was left with after constructing the table above: it is sobering—if not shocking and horrifying—to think how rapidly contemporary culture is sinking into these very evils. The younger generation perhaps has known nothing else to compare it to, but those with at least twenty years of adulthood behind them certainly recall a time when adult society was far more civil than it currently is. Displays of narcissism and arrogance that would have been shameful twenty years ago are now glamorized. High government officials are regularly attacked verbally and sometimes physically. Angry demonstrations and even riots erupt when financial pressures require higher taxes or lower pay and benefits. Celebrities notorious for illegal drug use and enslaved to various addictions receive public adulation. Indeed, crass hedonism increasingly rules the day: pleasure reigns as the ultimate good. For the majority, "I enjoy it!" seems to establish the validity of most anything. These evils have always existed, of course, but they have intensified alarmingly over the past generation.

One would expect such detestable evils to flourish only among those who make no claim to Christianity. But Paul's sentence does not end with this list of vices. He adds one final description of the people in view: "Having a form of godliness, but denying the power thereof" (2 Tim. 3:5). At least some of the people Paul has in mind are ones who make a pretense of Christian piety. Their conduct, though, manifests a lack of the life-transforming power of a true relationship with God in Christ.

What relationship should a God-loving believer have with such people? The closing words of verse 5 are plain: "From such turn away." Paul does not mean, of course, that we should not attempt to correct them; we noted already in Ephesians 5:11 that we are to correct such behavior when we encounter it. He does mean, certainly, what he also said in that same verse: "Have no fellowship with the unfruitful works of darkness." Those who wish to remain true to our Savior dare not condone or share the evil character of the age.

1 PETER 2:11–18

Peter, as well as Paul, calls for Christian conduct that is unlike the world. Beginning at 1 Peter 2:11–12, Peter commands abstinence from fleshly lusts and calls for "conversation honest [i.e., good, beneficial day-to-day conduct] among the Gentiles." He does not expect such conduct to earn the world's praise in the short term; he goes on to warn that the world will "speak against you as evildoers." Even the world, though, will eventually praise Christians' holy living, when "by your good works, which they shall behold, [they] glorify God in the day of visitation" (v. 12).

Peter goes on, then, through verse 18, to command six forms of Christian virtue, all positive, representing such good conduct before the world. "Submit yourselves to every ordinance of man for the Lord's sake" (vv. 13–16). "Honour all men. Love the brotherhood. Fear God. Honour the King" (v. 17). "Servants, be subject to your masters with all fear" (v. 18).

The call for obedience to civil authority is especially emphatic in this passage, and it illustrates the difficulty and subtlety that maintaining separation from the world often entails. Peter had earlier acknowledged that the world will speak against holy living as evil. Nowhere was this fact more apparent in the first century than in the matter of emperor worship. As an expression of political allegiance to Rome, citizens were expected to offer a pinch of incense at a pagan temple in acknowledgement of the emperor's "deity." Few if any would have thought that the emperor was truly divine; the rite was understood as merely a civil observance. But Christians wishing to be true to their Savior could not participate, bringing upon themselves the opprobrium and penalty of disloyalty to the state.

It is noteworthy, then, that against this backdrop Peter did not denounce the Roman government or call for political belligerence. On the contrary, he calls for obedience and even commands, "Honour the king." Worship, no, but honor, yes. Give the king not an ounce more than he is entitled to, but neither an ounce less. Today's believers, too, will find it necessary to walk fine lines between improper participation in the world's evils and improper antagonism against divinely ordained aspects of social order.

1 PETER 4:3–5

Is Peter's take on worldliness, then, purely positive? Does he list no worldly evils that believers must shun? No, Peter is not purely positive. The passage we just considered opens with a general prohibition against "fleshly lusts, which war against the soul" (1 Pet. 2:11), and in chapter 4 Peter lists specific negatives of worldliness that believers must avoid:

> For the time past of our life may suffice us to have wrought the will of the Gentiles, when we walked in lasciviousness, lusts, excess of wine, revellings, banquetings, and abominable idolatries: wherein they think it strange that ye run not with them to the same excess of riot, speaking evil of you: who shall give account to him that is ready to judge the quick and the dead (1 Pet. 4:3–5).

The emphasis here falls upon bodily indulgences to be denied, along with idolatry. We should not fail to note Peter's use of the world "abominable." The Greek word, *athemitos*, is rare, occurring in the New Testament only here and in Acts 10:28, where it refers to the impropriety of Jewish fellowship with Gentiles. Its most common meaning is simply "unlawful, illicit." Moulton and Milligan, however, quote a papyrus reference from 116 BC declaring that dead bodies are *athemitos* to certain goddesses.[5] Deities are not subject to laws, so lawlessness must not be the idea here, and Moulton and Milligan take the quotation as support for the rendering "abominable" in 1 Peter 4:3. Other Greek lexicons and several translations agree, translating "abominable" or "detestable." The point is that our Father's disapproval of idolatry is not bland or casual. He reacts violently against it, so any believer wishing to maintain intimacy with Him must beware of it and carefully avoid it. If the potential for idolatry in your own life seems only remote, perhaps you have forgotten that Scripture twice calls covetousness idolatry (Eph. 5:5; Col. 3:5).

MATTHEW 6

The sixth and final passage we will examine is Matthew 6, a beloved chapter from Jesus' Sermon on the Mount. The chapter opens with four relatively brief cycles of Jesus' forbidding a particular behavior patterned after ungodly culture, then requiring instead a contrasting behavior. The language is simple, following a pattern like, "Do not do such-and-such, like the so-and-so's. Instead, do the opposite." After these four cycles, a fifth topic is treated similarly, but at greater length and without the patterned language. These five topics are as shown in the following table.

[5] J. H. Moulton and George Milligan, *The Vocabulary of the Greek Testament, Illustrated from the Papyri and Other Non-Literary Sources* (Grand Rapids: Eerdmans, 1930). S.v. ἀθέμιτος, p. 11.

Verses	Behavior forbidden	Bad example	Behavior required
1–4	ostentatious giving	hypocrites	private giving
5–6	ostentatious praying	hypocrites	private praying
7–13	babbling in prayer	heathen	simple praying
16–18	ostentatious fasting	hypocrites	private fasting
19–34	preoccupation with material things	Gentiles	focus on heaven

Especially with regard to the first four cycles, two things are particularly noteworthy. First, the points of correction Jesus singles out are matters of religious ritual. Worldliness is not merely a matter of sensual indulgence of various kinds. Worldliness can include actions that appear to be very godly but are in fact nothing more than exercises in what John calls a worldly "pride of life" (1 John 2:15–16).

Second, Jesus emphasizes this disconnect between appearance and reality by singling out the hypocrites as those whom His disciples are not to imitate. The English word *hypocrite* derives from the underlying Greek word, which in that day's secular usage denoted a stage actor. It was natural for Christian writers to use the word for someone who displayed an outward piety as a mask to cover an ungodly heart or private life. The biblical usage of the word gives no reason to think that Jesus intends us to understand "the hypocrites" as a category of genuine but spiritually undeveloped believers.[6] Our Savior's denunciations in Matthew 23 of the "scribes and

---

[6] This is not to claim that a believer can never be guilty of hypocrisy. Indeed, even Peter and Barnabas fell into that sin on one occasion (Gal. 2:11–13; the word is rendered in the KJV as "dissimulation"). The New Testament uses the word *hypocrite* so

Pharisees, hypocrites" assert that they do not enter the kingdom of God (v. 13), will receive condemnation (v. 14), and are children of hell (v. 15). In case these descriptions leave any doubt about these people's spiritual condition, verse 33 should settle the matter: "Ye serpents, ye generation of vipers, how can ye escape the damnation of hell?"

The fact that hypocrites play up their religiosity often makes it more difficult for sincere believers to arrive at appropriate standards for their own living. When the hypocrites take care to dress in certain ways, and when they parade their avoidance of behaviors they mark as sinful and their practice of those they mark as righteous, those who rightly wish to avoid being perceived as hypocrites may incline toward completely different modes of living. It is important to observe, though, that Jesus does not command His disciples to avoid alms, prayer, and fasting. Motive and spirit come in for correction in these cases, but not the behaviors themselves. Only in the two cases where the bad examples are the Gentiles (babbling in prayer and preoccupation with material things) does Jesus' forbid the behavior itself.

Evident in this passage, then, are two different kinds of worldliness. Those who know nothing of God manifest many behaviors diametrically opposite to what is appropriate for Christians, while those who make a pretense of knowing God impart a spirit of worldly religious pride to behaviors that, in themselves, are right and proper. Jesus' true disciples must take care to identify and avoid worldliness in both of these forms.

---

negatively, however, that it seems clearly to denote a person who deliberately engages in hypocrisy as a settled pattern of life.

SUMMARY

At the risk of redundancy, but for reasons that will become apparent later, let us collect in one place the positive and negative points at which a believer's character or behavior are to stand in contrast to the world. The following table presents, in a categorized list, the ideas (not always the exact words) found in the six passages we have examined, in which a believer's lifestyle is contrasted either with that of the world or with his own lifestyle prior to salvation.

Category	Sin prohibited	Virtue required	Reference(s)
Bodily Appetites	sexual immorality	purity	Eph. 5:3; 1 Pet. 4:3; Titus 2:5
	drunkenness		Eph. 5:18; Titus 2:3; 1 Pet. 4:3
	gluttony		1 Pet. 4:3
	wild parties		1 Pet. 4:3
	lovers of pleasures		2 Tim. 3:4
Attitudes	inordinate anger	appropriate anger (?)	Eph. 4:26f.
	expressions of malice	kindness and forgiveness	Eph. 4:31f.
		sobriety	Titus 2:2, 6
		gravity	Titus 2:2, 7
	lack of self-control	self-control	Titus 2:2; 2 Tim. 3:3
		faith	Titus 2:2
	self-love	love	Titus 2:2; 2 Tim. 3:2
		endurance	Titus 2:2
		discretion	Titus 2:5
	despising good	goodness	Titus 2:5; 2 Tim. 3:3
		sincerity	Titus 2:7
	not brawling	gentleness, meekness	Titus 3:2

Category	Sin Prohibited	Virtue required	Reference
Attitudes Cont'd	pride		2 Tim. 3:2
	ingratitude		2 Tim. 3:2
	fierceness		2 Tim. 3:3
	recklessness		2 Tim. 3:4
	conceitedness		2 Tim. 3:4
Speech	lying	speaking truth	Eph. 4:25
	corrupt and immoral speech	edifying speech; thanksgiving	Eph. 4:29, 31; 5:4
	false accusation		Titus 2:3; 2 Tim. 3:3
		teachers of good things	Titus 2:3
		uncorruptness in teaching	Titus 2:7
		sound speech	Titus 2:8
	back-talking		Titus 2:9
	speaking evil of people		Titus 3:2
	boasting		2 Tim. 3:2
	blasphemy		2 Tim. 3:2
Relationships		love for family	Titus 2:4
	disobedience	obedience	Titus 2:5, 9; 3:1; 2 Tim. 3:2; 1 Pet. 2:18
		exemplifying good works	Titus 2:7
		pleasing master	Titus 2:9
		faithfulness	Titus 2:10
		submission to government	Titus 3:1; 1 Pet. 2:13
	without natural affection		2 Tim. 3:3
	unwillingness to reconcile		2 Tim. 3:3

Relationships Cont'd		treachery	2 Tim. 3:4
		honor for men	1 Pet. 2:17
		love for the brotherhood	1 Pet. 2:17
		fear of God	1 Pet. 2:17
		honor for the king	1 Pet. 2:17
Material goods	stealing	working and giving	Eph. 4:28; Titus 2:10
	covetousness		Eph. 5:3; 2 Tim. 3:2
	preoccupation with material things	focus on heaven	Matt. 6:19–34
Religious ceremony	abominable idolatries		1 Pet. 4:3
	ostentatious giving	private giving	Matt. 6:1–4
	ostentatious praying	private praying	Matt. 6:5–6
	babbling in prayer	simple praying	Matt. 6:7–13
	ostentatious fasting	private fasting	Matt. 6:16–18
Miscellaneous		behavior reflecting holiness	Titus 2:3
		caring for the home	Titus 2:5
		readiness for good works	Titus 3:1
	unholiness		2 Tim. 3:2

Perusing this list of matters of worldliness leaves at least one very strong impression: the Bible does not merely forbid worldliness and require holiness in vague generalities; our Father has spoken in detail about specific areas of our lives in which we are to keep ourselves unlike the world and develop likeness to His own character.

4

DISCERNING THE WORLD, PART 2:
THE NECESSITY OF APPLYING BIBLICAL TEACHING TO MATTERS NOT EXPLICITLY MENTIONED

We found in the previous chapter that the Bible says a great deal about the details of a Christian lifestyle "unspotted from the world" (James 1:27). Nevertheless, when we look carefully at our surrounding culture, we find ourselves equally impressed with the number of things that the Bible says little or nothing about. Some features and practices of secular culture not mentioned in the Bible commend themselves as perfectly innocent and appropriate to all but a tiny minority of believers—things such as hearing or playing in a symphony orchestra, working as a volunteer in a political campaign, or using a cell phone. At the other extreme, some commonly accepted cultural practices not directly addressed in Scripture are seen as ungodly by a large majority of Christians—things such as casino gambling or sexually suggestive rock concerts. Between these extremes lies a large group of cultural issues that are controversial among Christians. Examples of cultural practices that the Bible does not explicitly approve or disapprove include attendance at a movie theater, Sunday sports, games involving dice or playing cards, stock market investing, gender-mixed swimming, expensive cars, luxury homes, or handheld microphones for church music and preaching. One could easily list dozens or even hundreds of items that some Christians insist are worldly and others equally insist are not.

Evaluating elements of contemporary culture for their appropriateness within our Christian lives often raises the question of what to do when we find the Scripture silent on some specific issue. The alternatives range from inferring from that silence a full personal liberty, at the one extreme, to constructing, at the other, detailed do-and-don't schemes based on a variety of applications and inferences so that the Bible is viewed as supplying definitive and authoritative direction about any conceivable question of lifestyle or behavior. Both extremes are guilty of presumption: one presumes liberty while the other presumes to speak for God. Jesus rebukes those who attach too much authority to human tradition (Mark 7:5–13); Paul insists on liberty but warns against using it as an excuse for fleshly indulgence (Gal. 5:13). What we need is *discernment*, which Tim Challies helpfully defines as "the skill of understanding and applying God's Word with the purpose of separating truth from error and right from wrong."[1]

To fully explore a proper method of biblical application lies far beyond the scope of this book, but we must give it more than superficial mention. The present chapter will establish the necessity of application in general; chapter 5 will go on to develop principles for applying the Bible's teaching on worldliness to issues of contemporary culture that the Bible does not directly address.

AN ERRONEOUS VIEW

Are there large areas of cultural practice regarding which the Bible provides no guidance at all? We have already observed that there are, in fact, many issues for which the Bible provides no definitive teaching. The Bible does not establish definite rules about matters such as how much skin a believer's clothing may expose, what styles of music one may enjoy personally or use in church, what kinds of entertainment are acceptable, what kinds of cars honor

---

[1] Tim Challies, *The Discipline of Spiritual Discernment* (Wheaton, IL: Crossway, 2007), 61.

Christ, or what sorts of employment believers may hold. Some well-meaning Christians, citing the Reformation principle of *sola scriptura* ("Scripture alone," as opposed to Roman Catholic adherence to Scripture plus tradition), reason that since Scripture does not specify such details and we are forbidden to add tradition to Scripture, it follows that believers are at liberty of personal choice in such matters. Since God judges the heart rather than the outward conduct, the reasoning goes, insisting on standards that the Bible does not specify is a form of legalism. *Sola scriptura* means that the Bible is enough, so where the Bible says nothing, nothing needs to be said, and to say something anyway is to add to the Word of God.

As with most cases of error, this reasoning manifests a great deal of truth. Most emphatically, the Bible does say all that needs to be said about how to please God.[2] *Sola scriptura* is valid. The Bible is indeed enough; however, some Christians fail to do enough with the Bible. The Bible itself demands that we apply its teachings to matters beyond what it explicitly states.[3]

INDICATIONS THAT APPLICATION IS REQUIRED

Use of General Words and Expressions

We will observe first the use of the word *such* in key passages listing forms of good and evil. The catalog of pagan evils listed at the end of Romans 1 concludes with an assertion that even the pagan conscience knows "that they which commit such things are

---

[2] The Reformers certainly did not intend *sola scriptura* to affirm that the Bible contains everything one needs to know about everything. Doctors, lawyers, and engineers certainly need textbooks in their fields, and everyone must be able to perform basic math computations in order, for example, to determine whether he can afford some purchase, or to calculate a tithe of his income. The Bible contains little or no instruction in such matters, so it is not absolutely sufficient for *everything*.

[3] This is not at all the same thing as adding to Scripture doctrinal points such as the Catholic teachings of purgatory or the Immaculate Conception of Mary.

worthy of death" (v. 32). The opening of Romans 2 refers back to the list twice, with the same expression, "such things" (vv. 2, 3). The lists delineating the works of the flesh and the fruit of the spirit in Galatians 5 are both left open-ended by the expressions "such" and "such things" at the end (vv. 21, 23). If Paul had thought of these lists as comprehensive, he could easily have said "*these* things," which would not so clearly have invited the reader to broaden the lists with similar items. The word *such*, though, implies that Paul intends these lists as representative, not exhaustive. Yes, *such* could possibly be understood as simply emphasizing the moral character of the items in the list, but 1 Timothy 1:10, at the end of a list of evils, is unambiguous: "And if there be any other thing that is contrary to sound doctrine." This mode of presentation requires the reader to think about the character of the items listed and include in the list any other item of the same character. In other words, Paul not only *allows*, but *expects* the reader, as he encounters various circumstances in life, to expand the list to include items not mentioned.

Also noteworthy is the general nature of many of the items listed previously in the large table of sins and virtues that the New Testament explicitly lists in its discussions of worldliness. Of the seventy-five or so items listed, I found only about one-third that seem fairly specific, such as the evils of lying and stealing, and the virtues of gratitude and submission to government. The rest are quite general, requiring discerning application, such as the evils of loving self and hating good, and the virtues of loving family and doing good works. So even most of the matters of worldliness on which the Scripture speaks explicitly are themselves general in nature, requiring specific application in specific situations. For example, the Scripture says nothing about playing golf, and few would argue that the game is inherently evil. But some people's devotion to it amounts to loving pleasure more than loving God (2 Tim. 3:4). Determining whether one's own golfing habits are worldly or not requires discerning application of explicit but general scriptural teaching.

Key Passages

We will now examine three specific passages supporting the claim that the Bible not only allows but requires its readers to apply its teachings to parallel matters not specifically mentioned. We will take these passages in order of increasing relevance for our study. Consider first these words from Paul:

> No man that warreth entangleth himself with the affairs of this life; that he may please him who hath chosen him to be a soldier. And if a man also strive for masteries, yet is he not crowned, except he strive lawfully. The husbandman that laboureth must be first partaker of the fruits. Consider what I say; and the Lord give thee understanding in all things (2 Tim. 2:4–7).

If I may put it this way, this passage says more than it says. Paul makes simple statements about a soldier, an athlete, and a farmer. But when he goes on to say, "Think about this, and may the Lord help you understand," he makes clear that he means to communicate more than he actually says. Of course he could have gone on to explain exactly what he had in mind, but he did not. He left it up to Timothy first, and every reader since then, to infer not only the correct interpretation of these statements but also their application to his or her own life. He is not simply allowing Timothy to infer such application; his presentation requires it.

In Mark 2:23–28, the Pharisees ask why Jesus' disciples are violating the Sabbath by plucking ears of grain in order to have a bite to eat as they passed through a field. Jesus' response justifies this action by paralleling it to what David did when he and his men were hungry when David was on the run from Saul: they ate the showbread, which, under the law, only priests were allowed to eat. This Old Testament passage says nothing about Sabbath observance, but Jesus makes clear that, again, the passage says more than it says. Beyond recording that David and his men ate the showbread, it says something about how God's anointed King may deal with ceremonial regulations in exceptional cases of need. As with the previous passage, note again that Jesus did not merely allow such handling of an Old Testament text; He required it. His words "have ye never read?" (v. 25) fault the Pharisees for a defective reading of Scripture. The Bible said enough to justify the actions of Jesus' disciples on this occasion, but the Pharisees had failed to do enough with their Bible to recognize it.

The third passage to consider is 1 Corinthians 10:1–11, where, in the process of discussing the issue of whether it was permissible to eat meat offered to idols, Paul recounted part of Israel's experience at the time of the Exodus and in the wilderness. God brought all the Israelites out of Egypt and to Himself, yet He was displeased with many of them and allowed all but Joshua and Caleb to perish in the desert. This passage says nothing about sitting down to a meal in a Corinthian idol temple (cf. 1 Cor. 8:10), which was in that day a matter of simple social convention. But Paul uses the passage to warn his readers that they may bring God's displeasure upon themselves if they allow their bodily appetite to draw them into participation in demonic ceremonies (cf. 10:14–22). The Exodus and wilderness accounts say more than they say, and it is imperative for Paul's audience to grasp the full meaning and apply it appropriately to the cultural question at hand. Paul finds that the

Bible does provide guidance for the Corinthians' question, once he does enough with his Bible.

Because this passage about meats offered to idols in 1 Corinthians 8–10 is so relevant to our whole discussion, we must explore it in some detail. Once we gain a clear understanding of Paul's rather complex discussion in this passage, we will have a powerful scriptural model for handling a variety of contemporary parallels.

In 1 Corinthians 7:1, Paul begins to take up a series of questions that the Corinthians had written him to inquire about: "Now concerning the things whereof ye wrote unto me." In 7:25, 8:1, and 12:1,[4] Paul moves through this series of questions. Chapters 8–10 are his response to the question about the eating of meat offered to idols. The issue is multifaceted, based on the various situations in which idol meat might be eaten. A believer might have a meal in the actual temple facility (8:10), meat that he bought at the market (10:25) might be left over from an idol sacrifice, or he might be invited to a meal in a private residence where such meat was served (10:27).

A fascinating consideration about this whole discussion is that the Jerusalem Council has already prohibited meat offered to idols (Acts 15:29). Why does Paul not settle the matter by simply quoting the ruling? Clearly, instead of taking a simple approach that might be faulted as legalism—"We're not allowed"—Paul is exercising and calling for spiritual discernment.[5] Once the passage

---

[4] First Corinthians 16:1 and 16:12 may also refer to such questions; the commentators are not unanimous on the matter. Ben Witherington III, *Conflict and Community in Corinth: A Socio-Rhetorical Commentary on 1 and 2 Corinthians* (Grand Rapids: Eerdmans, 1995), 313; Anthony C. Thiselton, *The First Epistle to the Corinthians*, The New International Greek Testament Commentary (Grand Rapids: Eerdmans, 2000), 1317f.

[5] It is also possible that the Corinthians' question directly challenged the council's prohibition and that what Paul is doing here is defending it. In that case, referring

is clearly understood, it is plain that Paul does call for abstaining from meat that is known to be idol meat.[6] But he does not take the prohibition so far as to insist that no believer eat a bite of meat before first insuring that it did not come from an animal that had been offered in pagan sacrifice.

Why are such scruples unnecessary? Probably one factor is that the prohibition is a matter of human judgment rather than explicit divine command. Nowhere did the Old Testament or Jesus directly prohibit such eating. Full and accurate knowledge about the inherent nature of the idols and the meat provides another reason not to be over-scrupulous: since an idol is in fact nothing (8:4), it cannot defile the meat offered to it (10:19). How does Paul know these things? The Old Testament declares frequently that there is only one God,[7] and the impotence of the idols suggests that in fact they are nothing at all. As to the meat, Jesus taught that food in itself is incapable of defiling a person because, rather than entering the heart, it simply passes through the digestive tract, where, obviously, no moral operations take place for the food to affect (Matt. 15:10–20; Mark 7:14–23).

---

to the council's decision would have been pointless; the council would already be front-and-center in the Corinthians' question. A challenge by the Corinthians may have run something like this: "Don't you know that idols are nothing and that meats are incapable of defiling? How are we supposed to know where the meats we buy at the market came from? We can ask, but what if the butcher doesn't know? And what if we eat at some unsaved friend's house, who doesn't care where his meat came from? How are we supposed to know whether it's an idol sacrifice? This is really an unreasonable prohibition!" Such a challenge would perfectly account for the details of Paul's discussion in these chapters. These points could also have been raised as a matter of sincere inquiry rather than as a challenge, but Paul's opening warning against being puffed up based on knowledge suggests that, if not outright challenge, he has at least detected pride in their approach to the matter. Witherington (186f.) sees the situation similarly.

[6] This is consistent with the clear condemnation of the practice in Revelation 2:14, 20.

[7] The key passage is Isaiah 43–45, where our Father asserts at least a dozen times that He is the One and Only.

Building on the foundation of that knowledge, Paul reasons as follows. Beginning with the idol itself (and by extension the meat offered to it), Paul reasons that these physical objects entail no inherent reality that would cause defilement. On that basis, one might justify partaking of the sacrificial meat. However, another reality must be factored in: some people's consciences consider the idol or the meat to be impure, and when such a person follows the lead of the one who has knowledge, he or she ends up condemned by conscience and thus suffers spiritual harm. Chapter 8, then, makes the case that, even though there is nothing inherently wrong with the idol meat, abstinence is the course of action that best promotes the spiritual health of all. Of the three scenarios listed above (eating in the pagan temple, in one's own home, or in the home of another), Paul mentions only the first in chapter 8 (v. 10; he does not finish discussing that scenario until 10:14–24). This chapter goes as far as to establish two foundational points regarding the permissive view: it is correct in claiming that pagan deities do not exist and that meat sacrificed to them is morally neutral, but it is incorrect in failing to safeguard the consciences of those whose understanding is otherwise. These points are foundational to the evaluation of the other scenarios as well.[8]

Paul proceeds, in chapter 9, to deal with the related matter of his liberty and apostolic authority. Is he not free? Is he not an apostle? Yes, he reasons; therefore he may deny himself for the good of those God has called him to serve. But it is not merely a question of intelligent choice; Paul also expresses concern for his spiritual standing when he concludes the chapter with, "I keep under my body, and bring it into subjection: lest that by any means, when I have preached to others, I myself should be a castaway" (v. 27).

---

[8] Fuller development of the understanding reflected here appears in Thiselton (607ff.) and especially Witherington (186ff.).

What? A castaway?[9] Yes. Another point of reality to consider on the issue is how God feels about the matter. Does Scripture give any guidance on that question? Paul takes up this topic at the beginning of chapter 10. Israel's experience in the wilderness teaches us that one can in fact enjoy genuine spiritual privilege and yet greatly displease God. What sort of conduct is so displeasing to Him? In Israel's case, it was a matter of inordinate appetite for food (v. 6),[10] idolatry (v. 7), fornication (v. 8), tempting God (v. 9), and grumbling (v. 10). All the passages Paul is drawing upon hit points involved in the Corinthian situation: desire for certain foods (sacrifices at the pagan temples usually provided high quality meat), involvement in idolatry, fornication (which was practiced openly as part of pagan ritual), tempting God (Num. 21:5ff.),[11] and grumbling, which would be the natural response of those unsatisfied with Paul's direction about the idol meats.

---

[9] Space prohibits a discussion of just what sort of spiritual failure Paul has in view here. Of the six significant commentaries on my bookshelf, four interpret the statement as referring to Paul's salvation, (C. K. Barrett, Witherington, Grosheide, and, apparently, Fee) and two take it otherwise (Thiselton, Morris). None lists various views or provides extended support. Whatever Paul's intent, it is a failure serious enough to be avoided at all costs.

[10] The "evil" apparently lies in the people's discontentment with the food God did provide.

[11] "And the people spake against God, and against Moses, Wherefore have ye brought us up out of Egypt to die in the wilderness? for there is no bread, neither is there any water; and our soul loatheth this light bread." Paul refers to "tempting Christ," probably because this text shows that the people spoke specifically against God, and the discontentment they showed regarding their diet implies that they were not satisfied with the manna that God had provided. Jesus, connecting Himself with the manna, said that He is the living bread that came down from heaven (John 6:51; cf. 6:31, 6:58). So rejecting the manna and wishing for other food amounted to "tempting Christ." Paul similarly fed the Corinthians a diet of Christ (1 Cor. 2:1–2), and in this passage he is implying that this diet of Christ will preclude some of the meat eating they had enjoyed. As Israel "spake against God, and against Moses," the Corinthian church often resisted Christ's work mediated to them through Paul's leadership; hence the warning against tempting Christ.

Do you see what Paul is doing? Without saying *anything* about the Corinthians' issue of idol meats, the Old Testament says *a great deal* about it. Paul has done enough with his Bible, and he has found there God's clear direction for this cultural question.

Beginning in 10:14, Paul proceeds to make the case that meat offered to idols does, after all, include a spiritual dimension. And notice how he deals with things: "I speak as to wise men; judge ye what I say" (1 Cor. 10:15). He appeals here to the Corinthians' intelligence[12]—their ability to grasp the reality of the situation. To participate in religious ceremony is to fellowship with the deity. But wait; hadn't he said that the idol is nothing? Is he reversing himself? No, he reiterates, the idol is nothing, and the meat is nothing (v. 19). Behind the idols, though, are demons, and pagan ceremony (the ceremony, not the meat) entails fellowship with those demons. To participate is to set oneself in hostility to God; do we think we are strong enough to prevail (v. 22)? "All things are lawful," he goes on to say, apparently quoting a Corinthian slogan. With this permissive principle he appears to agree; he does not negate it. He does, though, set forth equally valid realities that must also be taken into account: not everything is beneficial; not everything edifies. That which is harmful or destructive has no place in a believer's life, regardless of whatever legal principles might be argued.

What about cases, though, where idol meat is eaten in private homes, involving no pagan ceremony? Paul goes on to outline cases making clear that where no ceremony is involved, there is no need for concern over the origin of the meat. Believers may purchase meat at the market without questioning its origin; meat itself cannot defile. Similarly, when invited to the home of an unbeliever

---

[12] The Greek word for "wise men" is φρόνιμος (*phronimos*).

where the meat may have come from a pagan sacrifice, one need ask no questions. If, however, someone calls attention to the fact that the meat has been sacrificed to an idol, then the believer is to abstain, as a matter of protecting the conscience of the one who apparently has an issue with it, or, as the case may be, as a matter of testimony to an unbeliever who, aware of prevailing abstinence among Christians, may think that the believer will appreciate this information.[13]

In summary, Paul's reasoning appears to be as follows. Wishing not merely to assert the decree of the Jerusalem Council against meat offered to idols, he says, "Let me explain the spiritual realities of the whole situation. Meat is not capable of moral defilement, so you don't need to verify the 'purity' of all the meat you eat. Any-time you know that the meat is from an idol sacrifice, though, you should not partake. Certainly you should not sit down to a ban-quet at the idol's temple, where you will commune with demons and provoke God's displeasure. And if at a private meal someone informs you that the meat is idol meat, you should forego your lib-erty in the interest of protecting any weaker brethren who might be spiritually harmed by your example, even though you yourself are not harmed at all."

Paul's evaluation of this case exemplifies the value of fully devel-oped knowledge coupled with love (1 Cor. 8:1–3). This knowledge includes both that of the Scriptures and that of our culture. We

---

[13] The fact that the word for the meat that Paul uses here means "sacred sacrifice" instead of the pejorative "idol sacrifice" used previously may indicate that he envisions this notice as coming from a pagan rather than from a Christian. His reference to the other person's conscience, however, more likely implies that the one serving notice is a believer—very possibly a new convert who has not yet made the shift to Christian vocabulary and whose conscience may well be especially weak. It is also possible, of course, that Paul's word choice is purely a matter of style from which we should infer little or nothing.

must allow the Bible to say all that it says on these matters—guarding against the danger of imagining that it says more than it does—and we must be able to make good judgments about our own spiritual needs, the needs of our fellow believers, and the effects that various courses of conduct are likely to produce. Of all our needs, the greatest is a true love for God and neighbor that gladly denies personal pleasures in pursuit of the glory of God that emerges when we act in His and our neighbors' interest, regardless of temporal cost to self.

5

DISCERNING THE WORLD, PART 3:
GUIDELINES FOR APPLYING BIBLICAL
TEACHING ON WORLDLINESS

The previous chapter's discussion of the Bible's own example of applying its teachings to matters not explicitly stated leads to several principles that provide guidance for the task of application. Our aim is to make full, accurate use of all biblical teaching related to worldliness, coupled with full, accurate knowledge of the cultural matters at issue. To the greatest possible extent, we want to avoid all these errors equally, with respect to both scriptural teaching and cultural reality: (1) failing to perceive what does exist, (2) imagining what does not exist, and (3) combining both of the previous errors by misjudging what exists. The basic principle that must constantly guide us is consistency across the whole range of scriptural teaching on the one hand and cultural reality on the other. But this consistency is not mechanically determined; wisdom and discernment are required, as we have already seen, for example, in Paul's appeal to the Corinthians, as intelligent people, to judge his teaching (1 Cor. 10:15). The number of matters to consider and the subtlety of many of them make our task challenging.

THE BASIC PREREQUISITE FOR SCRIPTURAL DISCERNMENT OF WORLDLINESS

Discernment is possible only when, as we see Paul doing in 1 Corinthians 8–10, we conform our approach to Christian living to the Great Commandments: we rank our neighbor's welfare as equal to or above our own, and we rank God's interests above all. "Me first" is a fleshly mentality that always blinds us to at least some of the moral realities of a situation, robbing us of the capacity to make sound judgments and decisions.

Solomon's admonition to guard our hearts (Prov. 4:23) raises a crucial point applying to the whole range of worldliness issues. Our growth in the knowledge of God will be severely stunted if we are unable or unwilling to control our hearts: to criticize and deny ourselves what our flesh loves, and to commend and require of ourselves what our flesh resists. "I like it!" is the worldly Christian's most powerful argument in favor of something (along with its brother: "I don't see anything wrong with it!"), and "I don't like it!" is the strongest argument against. It is instinctive, of course, to value our natural affections, and to demand complete suppression of that instinct would be unreasonable. Spiritual maturity, though, shows itself by not allowing instinctive like or dislike to settle the question of appropriateness. Instinct is as often fleshly as spiritual.

The mature Christian, then, deals with his instinct along lines like this: "I see that something inside me likes or dislikes this thing. Is that my flesh talking, or is it the new man in Christ? Let's put this thing to scriptural test and see how it fares." Such reasoning reflects Paul's admonitions, "Prove [the Greek word means "test"] all things; hold fast that which is good. Abstain from all appearance of evil" (1 Thess. 5:21–22).

In Philippians 1:9–11 Paul prays,

> And this I pray, that your love may abound yet more and more in knowledge and in all judgment; that ye may approve things that are excellent; that ye may be sincere and without offence till the day of Christ; being filled with the fruits of righteousness, which are by Jesus Christ, unto the glory and praise of God.

Notice that abounding love is the starting point of a process that expands to include insight and sound reasoning and then ascends stepwise through a series of purposes—love that abounds in knowledge and discernment leads to making excellent choices that lead to a Christ-empowered moral integrity that, in turn, ultimately glorifies God. Romans 12:1–2 states the case similarly: presenting our bodies to God as living sacrifices and experiencing renewal of the mind are prerequisites to being able to "prove what is that good, and acceptable, and perfect, will of God." Those who approach lifestyle questions with an intent to justify what they want are certain to err and, to the extent that they influence others, to lead them into error as well. Truth and edification can grow only from the root of abounding love—an orientation that finds its joy in selflessly serving the interests of others—conditioned by accurate knowledge and discernment.

Basic Facts to Keep in Mind

1. Not everything lost people do is a matter of worldliness that Christians must reject. A lost woman eats a bowl of cereal for breakfast and kisses her husband good-bye for the day. Obviously God does not expect Christians to avoid such behavior simply because lost people do the same thing. Let us again consider these verses:

> This I say therefore, and testify in the Lord, that ye henceforth walk not as other Gentiles walk, in the vanity of their mind, having the understanding darkened, being alienated from the life of God through the ignorance that is in them, because of the blindness of their heart (Eph. 4:17–18).

The points of the world's behavior that Christians must not mimic are those that display its vanity, ignorance, darkness, and alienation from God. A crucial point of knowledge that we must always pursue when evaluating a particular point of culture is why people behave so. Does a woman eat a bowl of cereal and kiss her husband good-bye because she does not know God? Is this the sort of behavior that God forbids, so that these actions reflect rebellion against righteousness? Obviously not; therefore we need not view such behavior as a matter of worldliness that we must reject. Strict isolationist sects go astray on this point, failing to distinguish between normal human behavior that interacts with God's world and His creatures consistently with His design and that which arises in rebellion against His holy character.

2. It thus follows that detecting the world requires discernment, not a mere list of taboos. Scripture provides enough information for us to define the world as a concept. It is impossible, though, to define the world in terms of precise descriptions of its manifestations in human behavior. I believe a friend of mine who serves in youth ministry hit on an important point when he realized that, as he said it, "You can't define the world; the world defines the world." Our adversary keeps an ever-changing kaleidoscope of attractions before our eyes, and as soon as we think we have a pretty good handle on a matter, it morphs into something different that is once again challenging to assess. Nevertheless, certain constants of human nature are at the heart of the world—"the lust of the flesh, and the lust of the eyes, and the pride of life"—and these problems are detectable with scripturally conditioned discernment combined with simple, self-denying honesty. Of course, not much discernment is required to detect the worldliness of something like blatant pornography, but detecting the full scope of worldliness would require infinite discernment. None of us will ever have enough, but we can all grow and develop in this vital area.

As we seek to grow in discernment, an important point to consider is the fact that cultures, and therefore some of the boundaries of worldliness, are constantly changing. A neutral aspect of culture may take on moral significance for a time and then resolve to neutrality again as the world moves on to some new expression of ungodliness. Styles of clothing and grooming provide good examples of this phenomenon. When I was a child in the 1970s, many conservative Christians objected to flared pants, wire-rimmed glasses, facial hair, and even floor-length skirts. The fact that today these are dead issues for the most part does not imply that these objections were misguided at that time; thoughtful believers recognized a cultural significance in their day that is no longer apparent to us. It is a mistake to impose the sensibilities of one culture upon other cultures, past, present, or future. Except where Scripture is clear on universal human issues, only those intimate with a particular culture are positioned to evaluate boundaries of worldliness with accuracy. Cultural distance always challenges and often hinders cultural discernment.

Fortunately, the only culture within which our Father requires us to keep ourselves unspotted from the world is the one—or the few, as the case may be—in which we actually live. From time to time we may have occasion to try to evaluate some issue within another culture, but the difficulties raised by cultural distance require us to be reserved and tentative in such judgments.

3. A believer's distinctness from the world should focus on matters affecting his ability to know God and make Him known, as He really is. This principle reflects the truth developed earlier that at the heart of the world lies ignorance of God. Since the world asserts itself to suppress the knowledge of God in Christ, a believer must be alert to cultural influences that hinder his or her ability to gain an increasing knowledge of the Father as He really is.

The phrase *as He really is* is crucial. Our adversary is quite content for us to think about God a great deal, so long as we do not think *correctly* about Him. The account of Satan's conversation with Eve, as punctuated in the King James Version, contains two sentences uttered by Satan, and God is prominent in both. Satan apparently knows that he cannot remove God from our consciousness,[1] so he asserts himself in every conceivable way to corrupt our concept of God's character. Asserting falsehoods about our Father is of course one way to produce such corruption, but another is to quietly conceal certain truths about Him. To grow in the knowledge of God as He really is requires us to develop an expanding understanding of *all* that the Scriptures reveal about Him.

As Satan is content for us to think a lot about God, as long as we do not think correctly about Him, so He is content for us to feel warm and fuzzy toward God, as long as we know nothing of true, life-changing intimacy with Him. Judas apparently fit right in with the other disciples in their personal attachment to Jesus even though he remained a greedy thief throughout those years of discipleship and ministry. Though Scripture parallels intimacy with God and intimacy between humans to some extent, intimacy with God is ultimately in a category of its own. Paul expressed a deep desire for such intimacy when he wrote,

> That I may know him, and the power of his resurrection, and the fellowship of his sufferings, being made conformable unto his death; if by any means I might attain unto the resurrection of the dead (Phil. 3:10–11).

Intimacy with God in Christ involves an awareness of the death of the old man and an inexplicable power at work bringing to life a

---

[1] Even the word *atheist* has as its root the Greek root for "God."

107

new man created in the image of Christ, hungering and thirsting for righteousness, loving God with heart and soul and mind and strength, and loving neighbor as oneself. Nothing short of such experience as a child of the heavenly Father is the true knowledge of God that the believer seeks to gain and to share, and against which the world fights tooth and nail.

A deliberately worldly lifestyle can never produce anything more than an illusion that we are growing in the knowledge of God. Further, that which hinders our own knowledge of God will also hinder our ability to lead others to know Him. It will erode our testimony to the lost and diminish our helpfulness to fellow believers. A good question to help us measure a practice's effect on our testimony to the lost is this: "Will this keep the unsaved from seeing God's true nature in my conduct?" Putting the question another way, we could ask, "Does the Bible lead me to hope that my nonconformity to the world on this point would convict a lost person's conscience about his or her sin?"[2] If we wonder, for example, whether we should wear only plain clothing, like the Amish, we can ask, "Will my wearing bright colors prevent people from seeing God in me? Does the Bible lead me to believe that the colors in my neighbor's wardrobe constitute a sin of which he must repent for salvation?" Surely we understand that wearing a shirt other than black does not manifest a rejection of God or somehow hinder our knowing Him or making Him known.[3]

---

[2] Notice the focus of this wording compared, for example, to "Would my conduct on this point tend to draw someone to Christ?" Framing the question in terms of attraction will lead us to imitate sinners, as we assume that people will find most attractive the things displaying their own nature. Coming to Christ, though, involves conviction of and repentance from sins. We must be sure that our evangelism draws sinners in repentance to the Savior, not merely attracting them to the same sins in ourselves.

[3] Of course, wearing clothing whose colors or color combinations offend social sensibilities within a given culture may well hinder one's effectiveness in making God known. I do not intend my statement to be absolutely universal.

If we wonder whether we should dress modestly, we can substitute immodesty in place of color within our questions, and the answer will be equally clear. The immodest dress of our culture is part of the package by which the world attempts to throw off God's laws requiring sexual restraint and fidelity.[4] Immodest dress is also a powerful means by which we can hinder our fellow Christians' ability to know God. An immodestly dressed woman in a church choir, for example, can ruin whatever spiritual impact the choir's music, or even the whole service, would otherwise carry. Immodesty on a Christian college campus can provoke constant sin, robbing its victims of some of their best opportunities in life to deepen their knowledge of God and intimacy with Him.

Questions of associations are often relevant to this principle as well. Conforming my appearance or lifestyle to that of a subculture known for its refusal to obey God's commands, even if I do not live entirely within that subculture, will greatly hinder my effectiveness in communicating God's true nature. By identifying myself as a Christian associated with that group, I will leave the impression that I do not believe God objects to that subculture's behavior and that no condemnation and judgment awaits it.

I do not mean to say, of course, that a believer who looks like any unbeliever is worldly. Well-developed discernment distinguishes between generic modes of dress and basic lifestyle that characterize the mainstream of a society regardless of moral character and those modes that are specific to various subcultures known for evil and deviance. Scripture does not require us to develop uniquely Christian forms of dress, for example. Peter was identifiable as a

---

[4] I realize that some people's desire in dressing immodestly is simply comfort; not all are equally motivated by sexual lust. But the cultural pressure behind the prevailing immodesty is undeniably sexual, and immodesty is therefore a sin for which we could reasonably expect the Holy Spirit to bring a lost person under conviction.

disciple of Jesus by his accent, not his clothing (Matt. 26:73). On the other hand, though, Ephesians 5:11 seems clearly enough to forbid us from adopting trends widely recognized as associated with indulgent or deviant behavior. So, while we need not dress or conduct ourselves publicly in a way that screams, "Christian!" neither should we dress or behave in any way that would leave people who know both our culture and our Bible sensing an inconsistency between our testimony and our conduct. It is not enough simply to assert that people should not worry about such things; we are responsible, as much as possible, to make choices that raise no such questions.

In any case where the effect of something on our ability to know God and make Him known is clear, the appropriateness of the thing is settled. Further, such evaluation provides a scriptural basis for our lifestyle convictions that is far superior to mere conformity to the expectations or convictions of others.

4. God does not intend a uniform level of cultural participation or isolation for all believers. Given our human limitations, no individual—except Jesus—is capable of fully making God known as He really is. Our differences in personality and training will enable some of us to understand and make known some of God's characteristics especially effectively, while others of us will do better with others. A variety of biblical evidence supports this claim. The prophets were very different from one another: Elijah was a rugged man of the outdoors, while Daniel served amid the opulence of royalty. Some prophets were priests; Amos was a cattleman. Especially striking is a comparison of John the Baptist's lifestyle with that of Jesus. While John was countercultural in his clothing, diet, and even his shelter, Jesus participated in the everyday affairs of His society. Something of God's purpose in all this becomes apparent when Jesus rebukes His generation for scoffing at both John and Himself: God calls to people, through His servants, in a wide variety of ways in order to leave them without excuse when they reject them all (Matt. 11:16–19). The fact that God appoints one mode of living for one of His servants does not imply that that mode is the only acceptable one for all His servants. We should expect the variety of spiritual giftedness among God's people to entail a variety of lifestyles as well—all within the bounds, of course, of biblical holiness and purity.

Paul followed a pattern of cultural participation and flexibility. Within the passage we discussed at such length previously, Paul explains:

> For though I be free from all men, yet have I made myself servant unto all, that I might gain the more. And unto the Jews I became as a Jew, that I might gain the Jews; to them that are under the law, as under the law, that I might gain them that are under the law; to them that are without law, as without law, (being not without law to God, but under the law to Christ,) that I might gain them that are without law. To the weak became I as weak, that I might gain the weak: I am made all things to all men, that I might by all means save some. And this I do for the gospel's sake, that I might be partaker thereof with you (1 Cor. 9:19–23).

Paul's life and mission are all about the gospel, and he does not want to place any unnecessary obstacle in any lost person's path to Christ. As the apostle to the Gentiles, his lifestyle does not feature Jewish elements that could imply that Gentiles must first convert to Judaism in order to be saved. At the same time, as a Jew who longs for the salvation of his own nation as well, he is careful to avoid giving any impression of disrespect for the law. Though this passage is in the form of testimony rather than command, Paul seems to commend to all who love the gospel a similar approach: cultural flexibility in order to avoid unnecessary hindrance of the gospel message. The gospel contains its own offense: the proclamation that all are sinners, under condemnation, and unable to merit any mitigation of eternal punishment under the wrath of God. Those who minister the gospel must avoid, as much as possible, adding further offense by attaching, or seeming to attach, unnecessary cultural conditions alongside the call to turn from sins and trust Jesus Christ for salvation.

It does not follow, though, that effective evangelism requires us to participate in the world's expressions of its alienation from God. Missionaries to jungle areas would not enhance the gospel by stripping, darkening their bodies with paint, piercing and scarring themselves, and joining in tribal warfare. On the contrary, the gospel message is best supported by a lifestyle in contrast to the sinful ways of the target audience. The missionary does well to adopt the diet of his tribe,[5] but not the sins. This very passage where Paul explains his cultural flexibility also manifests some limits to that flexibility: Paul would risk offending an unbelieving dinner host rather than damage a fellow believer's conscience (1 Cor. 10:27–29), and he does not join pagans in their idol ceremonies (10:14). As important as Paul considers avoiding cultural offense to be, even more important is avoiding disqualification before God for giving in to earthly desires instead of acting always in others' spiritual interest (9:27). Jude 23 expresses the idea vividly: "And others save with fear, pulling them out of the fire; hating even the garment spotted by the flesh." Whatever the exact reference of Jude's spotted garment metaphor may be, it is clear at least that even in rescuing sinners we must never embrace impurity.

---

[5] As much, at least, as morality and prudence regarding health permits—probably no raw meat, definitely no tainted water, and absolutely no cannibalism!

5. Worldliness is a problem for all, not just for some. This final general principle returns to a question raised at the outset of our study. How pervasive a problem is worldliness? We are now in a position to see that only one human being has ever lived for whom worldliness was never a problem. For the rest of us with our fallen flesh, in one way or another, to one extent or another, worldliness is a problem. If you are not Jesus Christ of Nazareth, the virgin-born, sinless Son of God, then you have a propensity for worldliness. We should expect valid application of Scripture in matters of worldliness, then, to confront and correct us at various points. If we find the Bible only affirming and never correcting us, we are certainly failing to do enough with the Bible.

Among those who know and love the Lord, then, worldliness should be less an issue for controversy and argument than a matter for mutual discernment and assistance. Never underestimate our adversary's resourcefulness. One of his most effective stratagems for keeping us from helping one another discern and overcome our worldliness is to keep us arguing about it. Some of us are certainly inclined to give the world too much place in our lives; others may be inclined toward such isolation from the world that we are unable to reach it with the gospel. As some of the boundaries of worldliness change within changing cultures, some will perceive those changes more quickly and accurately than others, but all of us will find our flesh attracted to some form of ungodliness, whether new or old. Since none of us has an infallible understanding of the issues involved, we need one another's help toward understanding biblical teachings and principles, accurately assessing the various aspects of our culture, and discerning appropriate levels of participation by Christians.

Of course, the moment one party rejects clear teaching of Scripture, such mutual seeking for truth becomes impossible. Those who refuse to be bound by clear biblical teaching, or whose retort to "The Bible says . . ." is "Well, I just feel . . ." deserve no seat at the table where sincere believers are searching together for truth. Whether inclined toward a more restrictive or a more permissive position, we must learn, contrary to the spirit of our age, to discount the value of our personal preference, since "how I feel" is only one small and secondary point of reality. The primary realities we seek to understand are these: what does the Scripture really teach, what morality is really behind what is happening within the culture, and what will the spiritual effects of the various available alternatives really be?

When we have heard one another's wisdom on such questions and recognized it as such, allowing it to correct our own folly, then we have a strong basis for respect regarding our differences. We will more easily assume that God will use our differences to maximize the progress of His redemptive plan. Few if any of us individually can rise to Paul's ability to be "all things to all men, that I might by all means save some" (1 Cor. 9:22). But collectively, God can use us to reach people of every kind.

Our differences can also serve to hold one another's tendencies toward error in check. An interesting pattern evident in the development of Christian doctrine in the early centuries of the church can provide direction for modern generations on the controversies we face. Take, for example, the common theological language we use to express truth about the incarnation of Christ. Jesus is the God-man, one Person possessing two natures. This is a theological formulation expressed by the early church, not a quotation directly from Scripture. How did the early church come to express the truth in these terms? First, various Christological heresies arose, such as that Jesus did not have a material body, or that Jesus was born as a mere human who became the Son of God at His baptism. In the process of refuting error, even those who held the truth found it difficult to reach full agreement on the exact nature of Christ and how best to express the Scripture's teaching in words. Over decades of time they labored at various church councils until something like a settled understanding arose. This is the pattern by which the core doctrines of orthodoxy have come to be expressed in creedal language: heresy, followed by a challenging and prolonged search for truth, resolving eventually into reasonably clear understanding expressed in reasonably simple language.

The results of such a search for truth have proved enduring because the truths themselves are unchanging. Matters of worldliness, though, do not submit themselves to such once-for-all resolution since they involve human cultures with their constant change. Still, the pattern is valid. Some, like Demas, definitely forsake the Lord in favor of the world (2 Tim. 4:10). Some fall into the opposite error of an asceticism that views a complete denial of basic bodily appetites and pleasures as a religious virtue (Col. 2:20–23; 1 Tim. 4:3). Among those whose commitment to Truth enables them to detect and avoid these errors, we can still expect to find differences of understanding and emphasis.[6] Instead of engaging in hostilities over these differences, we ought to view them as calling for debate and discussion aimed at resolving as many as we can and respecting those that we cannot resolve. Conference, not conflict, is what we need. Only when conference fails might conflict become necessary.

As the people of God, we owe it to our Lord, to ourselves, and to the lost of our generation to make such attempts toward resolving our differences regarding worldliness. Good starting points for

---

[6] Romans 14–15, a key passage on managing differences of conviction, expresses no expectation that all differences should be resolved.

this pursuit of harmony would be to open our minds to the likelihood that some of the positions we hold are not entirely correct, to search out and consider the reasons supporting those who disagree with us, and to require of ourselves rigorous support for any contentious position we determine we must take.

When and where can we start? The first attempt should not be too ambitious, or it is bound to fail. But can't we begin somewhere? Can't some pairs of otherwise compatible pastors who know they disagree in this area sit down for such discussion? If things go well, couldn't they invite more fellow pastors from their areas to join them? There is no telling what a powerful testimony for the gospel could emerge from such conferences and how great the benefits for the saints might be.

BASIC PATTERNS OF BIBLE APPLICATION

Though space does not allow extended development, we must not fail to consider at least some basic patterns to guide our application of the Bible to matters of worldliness.

Transferring the Bible's Teachings Directly to Our Culture

Major portions of Scripture apply directly to every culture. Many of the Bible's specific scenarios reflect the universal human condition, and these scenarios apply directly to every place and time. Probably no better example can be offered than Solomon's instruction to his son regarding "the strange woman" in Proverbs 5 and 7. Both in person and indirectly via a wide variety of media, the strange woman is alive and well today—and equally or even more deadly. Diligence in applying Solomon's somber warnings in these passages would certainly have a drastic effect on the media habits of a very large percentage of today's Christians. Examples of other topics for such direct application include truthfulness, drunkenness, gluttony, obedience to authority, and materialism.

Narrowing the Bible's Generalities to Our Culture's Specifics

A very common form of Bible application consists of recognizing that some specific point of contemporary culture is governed by something more general that the Bible says. The passage that provides the prime opportunity for this sort of application with respect to worldliness is Romans 12:1–2:

> I beseech you therefore, brethren, by the mercies of God, that ye present your bodies a living sacrifice, holy, acceptable unto God, which is your reasonable service. And be not conformed to this world: but be ye transformed by the renewing of your mind, that ye may prove what is that good, and acceptable, and perfect, will of God.

"Be not conformed to this world" prohibits every form of worldliness. The open-ended nature of the command obligates us to evaluate all aspects of our lives, distinguishing that which is holy and proper from that which exhibits the unholy elements of our culture. It is very likely that Paul intends this statement to serve as an all-encompassing introduction to the instruction that he develops from here through 15:7, covering a wide variety of issues.[7] But there is no reason to think that Paul intended the details of the following chapters to stand as an exhaustive list of worldliness issues; we must accept and obey the command as broadly as Paul expressed it.

As an example of something more specific, the Bible obviously does not directly address the issue of obeying speed limits. Both Peter

---

[7] It is worth observing that all of this instruction about behavior appears as an integral part of the epistle that provides the New Testament's premiere explication of the gospel. Loose-living Christians who wish to glory in the gospel as the ground of their liberty must recognize that "Be not conformed to this world" is, if not actually part of the gospel, at least its first application for daily living.

and Paul do, however, speak more generally about submitting ourselves to civil law (Rom. 13:1–7; 1 Pet. 2:13). Peter's wording leaves no loopholes, as he commands us to obey *every* government ordinance, adding that this is "for the Lord's sake." Without getting into questions that arise over whether the authority really intends the speed limits exactly as posted or whether there may be situations where the authority would actually prefer driving above the limit, this much seems perfectly clear: driving at speeds one fears might result in arrest, for no reason that the authority would accept, violates these commands. Behavior that produces fear of a valid arrest certainly is not submission.

Our thinking in this category of application can move in either of two directions. We may be reading our Bible and pause over a general command to consider whether we are obeying that command in the specifics of our lives, or we may be wondering whether some specific of our lives complies with or violates biblical teaching. Either way, Scripture requires us to connect the Bible's generalities with our culture's specifics. Examples of other topics for indirect application of this sort include choices regarding caring for aging parents and various uses of social media. The whole range of the communication arts comes under this category: our production and consumption of photography, film, music, graphic arts, and so on are all governed by the Bible's general teachings about communication. Since the world uses the arts to communicate its ungodliness so powerfully, the Bible's general teachings about worldliness are relevant across all types of artistic endeavor.

Expanding the Bible's Specifics to Integrally Related Issues
What the Bible teaches regarding some particular point implies similar teaching about everything integrally related to that point. Jesus expanded the commandment against adultery, for example,

to include the lustful look that precedes it: "Whosoever looketh on a woman to lust after her hath committed adultery with her already in his heart" (Matt. 5:28). Following this pattern, we must go a step further. If a woman dresses or adorns or carries herself with the intention of eliciting the sexual attention of a man, she is as guilty of the resulting heart adultery as he is. The fact that Jesus says nothing about her role in the matter does not put her at liberty to dress and behave however she wishes.

Similar patterns of application would apply, for example, to commands for obedience to authority and prohibitions against immoral speech. A command to obey implies a command to learn and remember what is required of me, as well as to insure that my influence on others is toward obedience. Prohibitions against filthy and corrupt speech prohibit my being a willing listener to such speech as well.

Imagine what sort of book the Bible would be if God outlined every last detail of every situation we might encounter. Such a tedious tome we would have! Rather, our Father expects us to exercise the wits He gave us and extend what He says on one point to include the whole package of surrounding factors.

Translating the Bible's Specifics to Our Culture's Parallel Specifics

Probably the most demanding sort of application we must make is that in which the biblical situation is different from yet similar to the contemporary situation. Sometimes the biblical situation does not even exist in contemporary culture. If we did not have Paul's inspired application of "Thou shalt not muzzle the ox when he treadeth out the corn" (Deut. 25:4) to the topic of ministerial remuneration,[8] reflecting the general idea that "the labourer is worthy of his hire" (Luke 10:7), we would probably be at a loss for any application to modern life beyond, perhaps, "Be nice to animals." Instructions regarding master-slave relationships fit into this category, the modern parallel, of course, being employer-employee relations.

Some Bible passages involve enough complexity to make the drawing of valid parallels difficult. First Corinthians 8–10 and Romans 14–15, for example, are sometimes cited as providing the program for dealing with the whole range of issues regarding which believers hold differing convictions. Both of these passages certainly involve the challenges that differing convictions create. Does it follow, though, that for every conceivable difference of conviction Paul would call for the same mutual respect and tolerance that he calls for in Romans 14–15 on the questions of diet and ceremonial observance?

The answer to this question is certainly negative. First Corinthians 6:9–20, along with 5:1–2, makes it plain that some in Corinth actually believed that their Christian liberty permitted them to engage in unlimited forms of fornication. Paul, of course, shows no respect for this conviction as he forcefully rebukes and refutes it. He treats the dietary and ceremonial issues in Romans 14–15 much differently, though. Elsewhere he makes clear that Scripture does not require the vegetarianism and ceremonial observances that some in Rome practiced. But rather than refuting these positions, as he refuted the Corinthian allowance of fornication, he calls for tolerance. Clearly, then, not all differences of conviction are to be handled in the same way.

---

[8] 1 Cor. 9:9 and 1 Tim. 5:17–18.

When differences of conviction arise in our day, how do we know which approach to take? When do we attack error, and when do we embrace and grant the right to hold a mistaken conviction? As we have previously discussed, the answers arise as we gain full knowledge of biblical teaching and cultural reality. Any Corinthian trying to justify his fornication will find himself completely lacking scriptural support. The slogans "all things are lawful" and "meats for the belly and the belly for meats" are not scriptural language but are instead human inferences regarding Christian liberty and God's creative design. Paul always has respect, though, for convictions that reflect some scriptural concern.

As we consider whether to treat some modern issue with the latitude displayed in these key passages, then, we must consider to what degree the modern issue is parallel. Is it an issue the Scripture is truly silent or ambiguous about? Or does the support for one position or the other fail to account for elements of Bible truth? Do the positions accurately account for the cultural realities as well as the scriptural teachings?

A good example of a valid modern application of the mutual respect and tolerance called for in Romans 14–15 would be some issues of Lord's Day observance.[9] Should a Christian eat in a restaurant on Sunday? Shop? Watch sports? Play sports? Work for pay? Is Sunday spiritually unique, or is it like any other day?[10] My impression is that today's Fundamentalists do a fairly good job of respecting one another's convictions in this area.

---

[9] It is not clear whether the special day Paul refers to is the Lord's Day or whether it refers to Jewish festival days.

[10] It is worth observing, by the way, that the "egalitarian" position Paul describes in Romans 14:5 is not one of *disregarding* the days thought special by some, but of *regarding* every day—apparently treating every day as sacred to the Lord. This position, then, as it might relate to Lord's Day observance, would not amount to failing to reverence that day but rather would insist on reverencing every day as the Lord's.

The issue of appropriate musical styles, though, does not appear to be a valid modern parallel to Romans 14–15—especially not the portion dealing with foods. As mentioned earlier, Scripture elsewhere declares the physical substance of foods to be morally neutral, since they do not enter the heart (Matt. 15:10–20; Mark 7:14–23).[11] This explanation clearly implies a categorical distinction between foods and music, since music both comes from the heart of the musician and enters the hearts of hearers. Sound as a matter of pure physics—variations in air pressure converted by the eardrum to electrical signals sent to the brain for processing—may be morally neutral, but sounds skillfully combined into musical patterns become avenues by which heart communicates with heart, and communication inherently involves morality. What we communicate is either consistent with God's character and the truth of His revelation and is therefore morally good, or it is inconsistent with those realities and is therefore morally evil. Little if any neutral territory exists in that realm.

First Corinthians 8–10, though, does appear to provide valid parallels to some views regarding music. A great deal of current controversy revolves around the question whether musical styles are in themselves morally neutral. For example, in a powerful essay on worldliness in music, Bob Kauflin, director of worship development for Sovereign Grace Ministries, declares, "It seems that God likes music of all kinds."[12] While for reasons given above and in

---

[11] Three other foods-specific verses sometimes misapplied to the whole range of lifestyle issues are Romans 14:14 ("I know, and am persuaded by the Lord Jesus, that there is nothing unclean of itself: but to him that esteemeth any thing to be unclean, to him it is unclean"), Romans 14:20 ("all things indeed are pure"), and Titus 1:15 ("Unto the pure all things are pure," written in a context dealing with Jewish false teachings and traditions certainly involving a dietary component).

[12] Bob Kauflin, "God, My Heart, and Music," in *Worldliness: Resisting the Seduction of a Fallen World*, ed. C. J. Mahaney (Wheaton, IL: Crossway, 2008), 70. It is clear in context that "all kinds" includes, for example, jazz and hard rock. Kauflin supports his claim with not a word of Scripture, only a quotation from Harold Best

the footnote below I find this claim untenable, let us suppose for a moment that it is true. It would not follow that God approves the use of all forms of music equally in all settings. First Corinthians 8–10 would require us to inquire further about how particular styles of music function within the culture. Does a musical style bring people into contact with the demonic realm? We must avoid communion with demons (10:20). In fact, Paul goes on to say that it is impossible to enjoy communion with the Lord while communing with demons (10:21). The implication is clear: God withdraws from fellowship with His people when they commune with demons. Does a musical style damage the conscience of some who subject themselves to it under the influence of others' leadership or example? We dare not wound our brothers and sisters; to do so is to sin against Christ (8:12).

---

arguing from the variety of cultures, races, and languages that the entire range of musical styles is necessary to capture the infinite fullness of God's glory (*Music through the Eyes of Faith* [San Francisco: HarperCollins, 1993], 67). Reasoning from the distinction between beauty, which is relative, and truth, which is absolute, Best argues that artistic style is incapable of expressing morality, concluding that no style is inherently incompatible with Christianity. Such reasoning is difficult to take seriously. Do today's more shocking forms of art featuring, for example, rotting food and excrement (see, e.g., http://www.nytimes.com/1998/06/10/arts/dieter-roth-reclusive-artist-and-tireless-provocateur-68.html or search the internet for "excrement in art") carry no inherent moral tone? Does a heart that can view such art with approval magnify God's glory in doing so? The very foundation of Best's reasoning is deeply flawed. Speaking of the philosophical starting point for his "musical pluralism," Best declares, with no mention of sin, "No matter how favorable or objectionable their music might be at first blush, it is of primary importance to understand that the music makers are honest-to-goodness people who must be loved first of all as such" (68). This statement is just one example of Best's consistent underplaying of depravity. While we certainly must love all people, artistic styles conceived by sinners to glorify sin are sinful (at least or especially during whatever period of time the cultural association remains strong), "the garment spotted by the flesh," that is to be hated even while one is engaged in evangelism (Jude 23). Best's claims to the contrary, though cogently argued philosophically, do not square well with Scripture. That such neglect of depravity has gained prominence among evangelicals is truly distressing. In spite of his unqualified approval of all styles of music, though, Best still finds weighty reasons to object to much if not most of what is happening on the Contemporary Christian Music scene, including its imitation of the world (159–82).

The idea that pagan music is unfit for Christian use is no mere knee-jerk reaction by aging traditionalists against the musical innovations of youth. Calvin Stapert shows that the church fathers of the first few centuries, regardless of their views on cultural accommodation in other areas, were surprisingly uniform in their rejection of pagan music.[13] Nor is the idea that rock musical styles portray a morality antithetical to Christianity confined to those who oppose rock. Robert Pattison, a secular connoisseur of rock whose 1987 work is timeless in its relevance, observes,

> Some dreamers have hoped to harness rock to propagate the values of transcendent ideologies. Populist Catholics sponsor rock masses, trendy educators produce textbooks using rock lyrics as a vehicle for inculcating traditional values, [and] various Protestant denominations commandeer the airwaves on Sunday mornings to broadcast uplifting advice larded with rock songs to make the message palatable to young ears. . . . But rock is useless to teach any transcendent value. The instigators of these projects merely promote the pagan rites they hope to coopt.[14]

[13] This claim is among his primary theses. Calvin R. Stapert, *A New Song for an Old World: Musical Thought in the Early Church* (Grand Rapids: Eerdmans, 2007).

[14] Robert Pattison, *The Triumph of Vulgarity: Rock Music in the Mirror of Romanticism* (New York: Oxford University Press, 1987), 137. Pattison writes elsewhere, "Which is not to say that rock is not a threat to organized religion. It is, but not in the crude sense of demanding a choice between Baal and Jehovah. . . . By forcing churches to compete on the basis of their ability to titillate the instincts of their worshippers, vulgar pantheism [as manifest in rock] compels the champions of organized religions to abandon their pretension to superior truth and thus turns them into entrepreneurs of emotional stimulation. Once God becomes a commodity for self-gratification, his fortunes depend on the vagaries of the emotional marketplace . . . as his priests and shamans pander to the feeling, not the faith, of their customers" (186f.). Pattison's thesis is that Rock is the modern, popular-level embodiment of 19th-century Romanticism, with its pantheistic philosophy—hence his expression "vulgar ('related to the common man,' not 'profane' or 'obscene') pantheism."

Let those inclined to believe otherwise seriously consider these things.

CONCLUDING THOUGHTS ON APPLICATION

I can imagine some readers sighing, "I can't think so deeply all the time; it hurts my brain. Surely God doesn't expect this of me. He just wants me to live in joyful liberty, right?" Paul considered the Corinthians fully possessed of the analytical skills he displayed in 1 Corinthians 8–10. Have the unprecedented information, education, and learning of our modern age so handicapped us that we are no longer able to think and analyze on a first-century level? Intense concern for detail is just what Paul commanded:

> See then that ye walk circumspectly, not as fools, but as wise, redeeming the time, because the days are evil. Wherefore be ye not unwise, but understanding what the will of the Lord is (Eph. 5:15–17).

The Greek word translated "circumspectly" means "accurately," or "carefully." It implies diligence in getting the details right. In connection with walking, it is appropriate to think of situations like crossing a river on stepping stones or making one's way through a minefield. Where you put your foot for each step matters, and you must be careful to insure that your footing is sound and safe before transferring your weight. If the reality of our lives were that our environment is safe, with no dangers lurking, then we would not need to concern ourselves with details in daily decisions. But Paul says the reality is just the opposite: "The days are evil." We can go through life thoughtlessly if we wish, but to do so is to be a "fool" and "unwise" and to miss God's will. The way that leads to life is narrow and filled with pressures; the way of easy living is the way that leads to destruction (Matt. 7:13–14).

Of course, it is possible to go to an extreme and obsess over minutiae. In Matthew 23:24, Jesus does not exactly condemn the Pharisees for filtering their drinks lest they inadvertently swallow a gnat (a tiny unclean animal),[15] but He certainly does not commend them for it, nor do we have any record that He ever did so Himself. Our goal in Bible application is to hear Scripture's whole testimony on a matter, in order to insure that what we so ravenously gulp down is not a camel (the largest unclean animal familiar to Jesus' audience) and to avoid renaming a camel a gnat in order to justify dismissing its importance.

As creatures in God's universe, we do not have the prerogative of designing reality to suit ourselves. Reality is what it is, as God and Satan engage in mortal combat over human souls. Why live as though life is easy when in fact it is not? Why live as though God has not given us a guide to safe passage when in fact He has? Yes, interpreting and applying the Bible demand our best efforts, sometimes making our brains hurt. Our findings often disturb our conscience and displease our flesh. Welcome to life as a Christian in this world as it is! And that, in fact, is just the question. The world most certainly is what it is—originally and fundamentally good, but now permeated with evil that is often exceedingly subtle. But what about us? Are we Christians or are we not? If we are, that welcome is not sarcastic but sincere, because the rewards of labor and obedience will infinitely surpass the costs (Heb. 12:1–2). Better a little hardship now than a great deal of loss or suffering forever, and a third alternative simply does not exist.

---

[15] The Pharisees' failure is not the straining alone but the combination of obsessing over tiny details of holiness while promoting the grossest disobedience to God on major issues of conduct.

6

DEFEATING THE WORLD:
ENABLEMENT FOR OVERCOMING

Along with warnings against worldliness and guidance for discerning it in the various aspects of our lives and cultures, our Father has given us instruction and hope for overcoming it. To motivate us to deal with the problem, He clearly declares what will be the cost of failing to do so. Just as the world itself is headed for no pleasant end, those who follow it, even believers, can expect to pay a steep price for conforming to it. Warnings without instruction and encouragement, though, produce only despair. Our Father has not failed to explain how we may overcome the world, and He also gives us the strongest possible encouragement: our Savior has in fact *already* overcome the world!

THE COSTS OF WORLDLINESS

Whether we know it or not and whether we like it or not, we are at war. Since the day Satan set himself against the Most High, a heavenly conflict has raged. Since the day Satan seduced Eve into eating the forbidden fruit and Adam joined her in the disobedience, the conflict has racked the earth as well. In pursuit of his objectives, our adversary lulls us into a sweet forgetfulness of his evil designs. Since most of the world is strolling down the path of destruction (Matt. 7:13–14), Satan's easiest successes come when people contentedly follow the crowd, oblivious to the reality of spiritual warfare.

The Scriptures, though, open our eyes to the truth. In Jeremiah's day, with the destruction of Jerusalem and the captivity of the nation looming, God warned His people in the starkest terms what lay ahead if they continued in their worldly ways. Lest we think that such warnings are irrelevant for New Testament believers, we must consider what Peter wrote to suffering Christians of his day: "For the time is come that judgment must begin at the house of God" (1 Pet. 4:17*a*). These words echo a passage in Ezekiel 9, where God sends forth His warriors to destroy the evildoers of Jerusalem, instructing them, "Begin at my sanctuary" (Ezek. 9:6). When the world is ripe for destruction, the first stroke of judgment falls upon the worldly among God's people, and Peter shows us that this pattern is not limited to the Old Testament.

"But haven't we been saved?" someone may counter. Certainly, those who have heard and understood the gospel, repented, and placed their faith in Christ's atoning work are saved. But it is important to note that our salvation is salvation from our sins, not just from the consequences of our sins. God challenged His Old Testament people on just this point:

> Will ye steal, murder, and commit adultery, and swear falsely, and burn incense unto Baal, and walk after other gods whom ye know not; and come and stand before me in this house, which is called by my name, and say, We are delivered to do all these abominations? (Jer. 7:9–10).

If God considered it absurd for His Old Testament saints to reason that He had delivered them from enemy nations in order to permit to them to do abominable things, on what basis would we think that New Testament saints have a greater license for sin? Does New Testament redemption accomplish a lesser degree of deliverance than Old?

Most Americans alive today have never experienced or even witnessed truly severe large-scale suffering. Thus it is difficult for us to feel the gravity of the danger that our worldliness is bringing upon us. A good starting point for considering how to overcome the world is to attend to what is at stake if we do not. I encourage you to read Jeremiah 19 as an example of how our Father deals with His people who refuse to abandon their worldliness. In this passage God declares through Jeremiah that He is about to do something to Jerusalem that will make the ears of everyone who hears about it tingle. The chastening will include a siege by a foreign army that will reduce Jerusalem to such a state of starvation that people will actually eat the flesh of their children and friends in an attempt to survive.

Our instincts recoil from even thinking about such a horror, but our Father has told us this because He wants us to think about it. Can you begin to imagine what it must have been like for those people, as their children and neighbors succumbed to starvation, to flay their corpses and make meals of the remains? Think of your child or sibling or parent or friend. Could you ever be hungry enough actually to put your fork into a piece of his or her flesh, put it into your mouth, chew it up and swallow it? This is really what God's Old Testament people brought upon themselves by refusing to repent of their worldliness, and nowhere does the New Testament exempt worldly believers today from the threat of such horror. A pretribulation Rapture does not eliminate the possibility of severe suffering for believers, especially the disobedient. True believers will never be under God's wrath as the world will (1 Thess. 5:9), but chastening for purification can be extremely painful (Heb. 12:11). If this is what our Father must do to deliver His people from the world, then this is what He will do, for He is determined that whatever it takes, not one who is truly His will ultimately perish with the world.

A passage like this, by the way, provides a good test of whether we know God as He really is. If our knowledge of God does not include a place for—and even a love for—our Father's stern response to the deliberate worldliness of His people, then our knowledge and love of Him are defective, and we had better search the Scriptures more carefully as we live for Him in this world and prepare to give account of ourselves to His Son in the next.

How much better it will be for us to yield obedience to our Father's commands now, so we can enjoy His blessings! In fact, the Ezekiel 9 passage referred to above includes God's instructions to one of His destroyers first to

> go through the midst of the city, through the midst of Jerusalem, and set a mark upon the foreheads of the men that sigh and that cry for all the abominations that be done in the midst thereof. And to the others he said in mine hearing, Go ye after him through the city, and smite: let not your eye spare, neither have ye pity: slay utterly old and young, both maids, and little children, and women: but come not near any man upon whom is the mark (Ezek. 9:4–6a).

Any worldly believer today who will turn from his worldliness and begin pursuing a life of true holiness can be sure of God's special care if and when a day of judgment and chastening falls upon the church.

We should not think, though, that the only danger of worldliness is the risk of earthly destruction and suffering of epic proportions. Such an end may or may not come upon any given generation of worldly Christians; judging historically, the odds are certainly in favor of our escaping it. Other damaging consequences of worldliness, though, are inescapable. While we may or may not suffer physically on this earth, every believer will give account of himself to God at the judgment seat of Christ, and Paul does not hesitate to apply the word *terror* to that event (2 Cor. 5:9–11; cf. Rom. 14:10–12).

The spiritual consequences of worldliness, though, are not limited to the next life. To the extent that we are worldly, we cannot know intimacy with our heavenly Father. In a well-known passage Paul warns the Corinthians against association with unbelievers in their sinful ways. The passage concludes with this command and promise:

> Wherefore come out from among them, and be ye separate, saith the Lord, and touch not the unclean thing; and I will receive you, and will be a Father unto you, and ye shall be my sons and daughters, saith the Lord Almighty. Having therefore these promises, dearly beloved, let us cleanse ourselves from all filthiness of the flesh and spirit, perfecting holiness in the fear of God (2 Cor. 6:17–7:1).

The blessedness of intimacy with our heavenly Father is conditioned upon our separating ourselves from the world in pursuit of holiness springing from a heart that is properly fearful of coming under our Father's frown. The fact that we are fully "accepted in the beloved" (Eph. 1:6) does not eliminate the possibility of our forfeiting the full blessing of our Father's intimate presence with us by aligning our affections with His enemies instead of with Him

(1 Cor. 10:5–6; 2 Cor. 6:14–18; James 4:4–10; Rev. 2:20–23).[1] John Piper, in his foreword to *Worldliness*, expresses this idea winsomely: "In the end, the sum of all beauty is Christ, and the sin of all worldliness is to diminish our capacity to see him and be satisfied in him and show him compellingly to a perishing world."[2] Though I do not wish to identify myself with the whole package of Piper's philosophy of the Christian life,[3] I do find in these words a key idea I am endeavoring to communicate in this book: worldliness prevents our knowing God and making Him known, as He really is. To the extent that we are worldly, our failure in these crucial aspects of the Christian life is inevitable.

The damage of worldliness, however, extends beyond our own growth in grace. God is zealous for the holiness of His name, and He does not take lightly the damage that the worldliness of His people does to His reputation. Scripture is clear: the priests and people of Israel were not to conduct themselves in any manner that would discredit God's holy name (Lev. 18:21; 19:12; 20:3; 21:6;

---

[1] This is not to claim that any believer who displays the least taint of worldliness knows nothing of God's intimate presence. The God Who knows the heart can see and respond to undivided affection even where, in ignorance or weakness, one's conduct is of mixed quality—and whose isn't? The believer who deliberately rejects holiness in favor of worldliness, though, should expect no enjoyment of his Father's smiling presence until he repents.

[2] John Piper, "Foreword," in *Worldliness*, ed. Mahaney, 13. I do not believe, though, that this statement with its subjective focus exhausts the problems of worldliness. Worldliness has objective dimensions as well, such as disobedience to God's Word and violation of His character.

[3] See John Piper, *Desiring God: Meditations of a Christian Hedonist,* rev. ed. (Colorado Springs: Multnomah, 2011). There is a fine line, yet all the difference in the world, between pursuing the glory of God in the pleasures that He chooses for me as I develop scriptural intimacy with Him, and presuming that I glorify God by calling Him the object of my self-chosen pleasures. Piper clearly intends the former, but I fear that he has subtly overplayed the Bible's teaching on pleasure in a manner that has contributed to the fall of many believers, under the influence of our narcissistic culture, into the latter.

22:2, 32), and God was displeased with them when they profaned His name among the nations (Ezek. 36:20, 21, 23).

Discredit to God's name is one of the products of worldliness among today's Christians. A book mentioned earlier, *Rapture Ready!*, provides a case in point. The author is an incisive critic of evangelical Christianity's borrowing from practically every aspect of contemporary pop culture. As a humanist, his unbelief strongly colors his assessment: to him the gospel itself is foolishness. He aims a large portion of his ridicule, though, at those who, in the name of serving God, pursue the pleasures and values of pop culture as though they had intrinsic worth or without seeing how they contradict what Evangelicals claim to believe. Of course, Christians should expect unbelievers to mock, but we must avoid giving them just cause to mock. We defame our Father's name when we combine shallow teachings on what the world knows are deep subjects with deep attraction to what the world knows are shallow pleasures.

THE CURE FOR WORLDLINESS

A lifestyle that repudiates worldliness, though, is no easy one. It crosses our flesh, and it crosses our culture. It requires us to recognize the conflict that rages and the sure destruction of the multitudes that surround us, and it requires us to exert ourselves unwaveringly against unwavering opposition. Jesus has such a picture in mind when He tells His disciples, "In the world ye shall have tribulation: but be of good cheer; I have overcome the world" (John 16:33*a*).

Thank the Lord, it is not up to us to win this battle and deliver ourselves from the world. Our Savior has accomplished for us what we would never be able to do for ourselves. He not only overcame the world Himself; according to Galatians 1:4, He rescued us from it. It does not follow, though, that our role is entirely passive. We, too, overcome the world.

> For whatsoever is born of God overcometh the world: and this is the victory that overcometh the world, even our faith. Who is he that overcometh the world, but he that believeth that Jesus is the Son of God? (1 John 5:4–5).

If overcoming the world required us to agonize on our knees for hours of daily prayer, or to memorize the whole New Testament word-perfectly, or never to succumb to our adversary's seduction, or never to fail to seize an opportunity to evangelize the lost, we would have reason to despair. But God has made it as simple as possible. Our Savior has done what is impossible for us: He has judged the prince of this world and has overcome the world. He has rescued us from the alienation from God and the hostility toward Him that characterize the world that is dead in sin, bringing us to life and seating us with Himself in God's very presence in heaven (Eph. 2:5–6). He has further taken up residence in our hearts in the person of the Holy Spirit, Who empowers our victory over the flesh (Rom. 8:5–11). John is telling us in the passage quoted above that victory over the world requires simply that we believe the truth about Jesus as God's Son. If we believe this truth and embrace it as our own, we will naturally feed this faith by regular intake of Scripture, received in the same faith.

When we read in Scripture that fornication and drunkenness and covetousness and lying are forms of worldly depravity that bring the lost to destruction, we will believe it, not dismiss it. When we read that our Father has set us apart as a holy people for Himself, intending to bless us beyond imagination if we obey Him, we will believe it, not dismiss it. When we doubt that the Sovereign of heaven could do so much for such worms as ourselves, we will remember that Scripture testifies that we have been baptized into the body of Christ and made joint-heirs with Him of all God's creation—with the indwelling Spirit given as the down-payment—and we will believe it as the bedrock on which to base our daily living, not dismiss it as some pie-in-the-sky thing that is powerless to overcome the lust or pleasure of the moment. The hymn captures it: "Faith is the victory that overcomes the world."

There is hardly a better passage for this world-overcoming faith to rest itself upon than Jesus' high-priestly prayer for His disciples in John 17. In this passage we learn that our very lives consist of knowing God and Christ (v. 3), and our Father has given us to His Son "out of the world" (v. 6). And yet our Savior is sympathetic with our predicament while we remain "in the world" (vv. 11, 15). He declares that, like Himself, we are "not of the world" and therefore are hated by the world (vv. 14, 16), and He asks His Father to protect us (vv. 11, 15). He also prays for our evangelistic mission to the world (v. 18), reminding us of God's intention for Old Testament Israel in this regard. One of the things this conviction will do for us is temper our tendencies toward carnal division[4]

---

[4] Scripture does not forbid division among professing Christians; it actually commands it in certain cases. The delicate balance between maintaining the separation commanded on the one hand and the unity commanded on the other is very similar in kind to many other necessary balance points in Christian living. For example, the fact that one is prone to gluttony does not imply that he should not eat at all. God intends us to enjoy eating as necessary, without overeating. Similarly, God intends us to enjoy the fruits of separated living without overzealously enforcing personal standards that violate the unity of God's people around the Bible's clear teachings on doctrinal truth and personal conduct. Unity of spirit among people who agree about everything will not impress the world as supernatural, nor, on the other hand, will a mere organizational unity that thinly masks a fundamental confusion of perspective and purpose and fails to temper carnal strife. A fair indicator that we have positioned ourselves appropriately will be that, based on scriptural considerations, we maintain unity at some points where our nature inclines to separate, while on the other hand we separate at some points where our nature inclines toward unity. In any aspect of Christian living, the one who never consciously allows God's Word to override his natural preference is certainly in some kind of error.

and strife since God intends the unity of His people to serve as a testimony to the world of the reality of Jesus' saving work (vv. 21, 23). One of the most effective antidotes to worldliness is a deep-seated conviction that the world is our mission field, not our playground. Do we believe all this? If we do, we are in the process of overcoming the world, and the deeper our conviction grows, the greater victory we will know.

All the means of grace that God has provided—the indwelling Spirit, Scripture, prayer, and fellowship with other believers—contribute to our victory over the world. Among the variety of ways we can avail ourselves of these means, no activity is more important in our battle against the world than our seeking to master the whole of Scripture, under the guidance of the Spirit Who inspired it. Our Father has given us an extended body of revelation, not just a few notes, in order to provide a well-rounded understanding of the complexity of His being and of His dealings with His creatures. This study has emphasized repeatedly the importance of knowing God as He really is. One of the major contributors to prevailing worldliness among God's people is a seriously defective understanding of His character and His ways revealed in the Bible.

Many Christians' use of Scripture is limited to occasional reading of favorite passages. If they read larger portions of Scripture at all, their approach is superficial, gliding along the surface until some familiar segment strikes them with a sense of blessing or comfort or instruction. Mature handling of Scripture, though, regularly goes much further. Unfamiliar or challenging passages call forth serious effort in reading. That effort often brings to light aspects of God's character and ways that rebuke and threaten our self-secure lifestyles (as does the Jeremiah 19 passage mentioned above). Such passages, no less than the pleasant ones, demand our faith and submission, coupled with gratitude and deeper love for Him Whose love for us is deep enough to be as tough as necessary to secure our eternal joy in Him. Such use of Scripture, though, is completely foreign to many Christians. They never do it themselves, and their pastors and teachers never minister to them in such a mode.

Really, now, can we possibly justify knowing more about and identifying better with the lives of current celebrities than with the lives of men and women of the Bible? How is it that we can watch a movie and experience all the emotions of the various characters but never find ourselves moved by the stories of Scripture? Something is drastically wrong. Sure, the Bible lacks the full-color visual element, but the films lack the moving power of the Spirit! The films, however, do not lack spiritual power. All too many of them are backed by the power of the evil spirits wooing us to destruction. Can we not see that it is high time to disconnect from Hollywood and get connected to the Holy Word?

In the absence of such exposure to and embrace of the whole Bible, believers default to a mode of living that takes its cues from the culture, and worldliness is the inevitable result. The believer who wishes to replace his appetite for the world with an appetite for the Word can do no better than to undertake a deep and meditative study of the first Psalm:

> Blessed is the man that walketh not in the counsel of the ungodly, nor standeth in the way of sinners, nor sitteth in the seat of the scornful. But his delight is in the law of the Lord; and in his law doth he meditate day and night. And he shall be like a tree planted by the rivers of water, that bringeth forth his fruit in his season; his leaf also shall not wither; and whatsoever he doeth shall prosper. The ungodly are not so: but are like the chaff which the wind driveth away. Therefore the ungodly shall not stand in the

judgment, nor sinners in the congregation of the righteous. For the Lord knoweth the way of the righteous: but the way of the ungodly shall perish.

Where do our affections lie? If we imitate the ungodly, the sinners, the scornful, we can expect to suffer with them. If on the other hand we love God's Word and make it our constant meditation, we will find the Scripture correcting our faults in order to deliver us from such suffering. We will not be like the self-defensive lawyer of Luke 10:29, but we will receive correction like the wise man of Proverbs 9:8. In response, the Spirit of God will assure our hearts of our Father's deepest blessings, no matter what challenges or difficulties He may appoint us to undergo.

What does it mean to meditate on God's Word day and night? Obviously the meaning cannot be that we never think about anything except the words of Scripture. It must mean at the very least, though, that we do not approach any issue in life without considering what the Bible has to say about it. Only to the extent that specific teachings of Scripture control our minds as we choose our music and entertainment, as we shop for our clothes, as we engage in and evaluate worship and preaching, as we surf the internet, and as we pursue all the other aspects of life on this earth, can we please our Father and expect the blessing promised in the first Psalm. And when the heart is right, such submission to Scripture is no drudgery; David calls God's law his delight (v. 2). How could we *not* delight in God's Word when we believe that it provides us the key to escape this present evil world and the destruction that is sure to come upon it?

Until our Father provides us the blessed enablement to believe and obey all that He has revealed to us, though, we have no possibility of experiencing the full measure of what it is to be His own choice people, reveling in the glory of knowing Him and His Son and sharing in their eternal life (John 17:3). For such glorious treasure the trinkets of this passing world are a poor substitute indeed. May our Father so revive our hearts that we increasingly learn to see the world for what it is and gladly turn away, so that we may embrace the One Who has redeemed us to Himself. "And this is the victory that overcometh the world, even our faith" (1 John 5:4).

CONCLUSION:
WORLDLINESS AND CHRISTLIKENESS

Our study up to this point has emphasized knowing God and making Him known, as He really is, as the motive behind the believer's refusal to conform to the world. This emphasis is vital. Without it the Christian's holiness is likely to be pharisaical and self-exalting—in other words, no holiness at all.

A closely related scriptural emphasis provides for our study a fitting note of conclusion. Every believer is destined for conformity to the image of Christ:

> Whom he did foreknow, he also did predestinate to be conformed to the image of his Son (Rom. 8:29).

> When he shall appear, we shall be like him; for we shall see him as he is (1 John 3:2).

Attainment of Christlikeness in the glorified state is not a sudden lurch into a completely new mode of existence; it is the culmination of a process of spiritual growth that unfolds throughout the believer's earthly life: "We all, with open face beholding as in a glass the glory of the Lord, are changed into the same image from glory to glory" (2 Cor. 3:18).

Peter connects our conformity to the divine image with our separation from the world, writing that God has promised that believers will be "partakers of the divine nature, having escaped the corruption that is in the world through lust" (2 Pet. 1:4). Christlikeness and worldliness, then, are polar opposites. To the extent that one is true of us, the other is false.

Herein lies the most powerful incentive to shun worldliness. The world is certainly evil, and its destiny is certainly fearful. But negative motivations, valid as they are in their proper place, are never sufficient to produce living that truly honors God. Is our Father glorified when we choose obedience to Him as the least of life's evils?

"Imitation is the sincerest form of flattery."[1] We observe this phenomenon in everyday life: you can tell a lot about who or what someone loves by watching who or what he imitates—or at least tries to. High school athletes imitate their favorite professionals. Business people pattern their careers after high-profile executives. Musicians and artists must establish their individual styles, yet they, too, adopt models of success on which to base their work.

Imitation, though, is not always conscious and intentional. We imitate instinctively, often without stopping to think about what motivates us to do what we do. Children are great observers and imitators, as many humorous or touching photos and videos attest. The phenomenon does not seem to disappear with age. Peer pressure is a huge influence on teenagers, and "keeping up with the Joneses" is a lifetime pursuit of many adults. It seems that God has placed in the human psyche a healthy impulse toward community that depends, in part, on people's inclination to unite around shared values and experiences. This is how culture— good or bad—develops and persists. As human beings, then, we will imitate others; as Christians we must move beyond instinct and consciously choose right examples to imitate, lest, like Old

---

[1] The familiar quotation originated with Charles Caleb Colton, 1820.

Testament Israel, we damage ourselves and fall under our Father's frown by living like the world. We dare not forget our Savior's warning: "That which is highly esteemed among men is abomination in the sight of God" (Luke 16:15).

Scripture does not leave us without direction about our choice of patterns to imitate. Jesus has set an example for us, and our Father commands us to follow that example (1 Pet. 2:21). To help us with the difficulty of patterning our lives after that of a Man Who lived long ago and far away, God has implanted His Spirit within us, and He ordains and enables spiritual leadership in every generation. He commands those leaders to set a right example for their flocks to follow,[2] and He commands the flocks to follow.[3] Even among believers with no official leadership positions, setting and following healthy examples is commended and commanded.[4]

Perhaps the warmest passage commanding Christlikeness appears in Ephesians 5:1–2, near the center of the long exhortation against worldliness that we examined back in chapter 3.

> Be ye therefore followers of God, as dear children; and walk in love, as Christ also hath loved us, and hath given himself for us an offering and a sacrifice to God for a sweetsmelling savour.

We have already noted how children love to imitate, which is the root idea of the Greek word here translated "followers." We can begin to feel the warmth of Paul's exhortation if we imagine some-

---

[2] 1 Tim. 4:12; 2 Tim. 1:13; Titus 2:7; 1 Pet. 5:3.

[3] 1 Cor. 4:16; 11:1; Phil. 3:17; 2 Thess. 3:7; Heb. 13:7.

[4] Phil. 3:17; 1 Thess. 1:7; 2:14. To assist us further, our Father has also placed in Scripture a wealth of negative examples, along with commands not to follow those. First Corinthians 10:6–11, highlighting Israel's disobedience in the wilderness, is one of the most notable such passages.

thing like a Norman Rockwell painting in which a father and son beam as the man presents the boy with a new ball cap or a fishing rod or a hunting jacket that is just like Dad's. If the picture sounds artificial or corny, it is only because our culture is on the verge of losing the relationship of love and affection that ought to exist between parents and children. When a child knows he or she is loved, though, that sincerest form of flattery comes straight from the heart. "What would you like to be when you grow up, sweetheart?" may well receive the answer, "Mommy, I want to be just like you!"

We need not lament the fact that the child eventually outgrows the tenderness of this inclination to imitate the parent. After all, the parent is a sinner, and furthermore, God has most likely appointed for the child a role in life different from the parent's. Further, the child's imitation is generally limited to superficial matters. Grown children often do take their parents as role models in more profound matters of life, right on through adulthood, whether or not they are conscious of it. Again, those most likely to choose consciously to imitate a parent throughout life are those who are conscious of the parent's love.

As believers, then, we have every reason to choose consciously to pattern ourselves after our heavenly Father and after His Son, Whom He gave as our example. What greater love can anyone know than the Father's love poured out upon His children? What sin or failure in the Godhead would justifiably alienate our affections? What attribute of Deity fails to commend itself as worthy of our emulation? What goal in life is more worthy of our aspirations and exertions than to be like Christ? What goal in life is more likely to elicit our Father's approval and His supernatural enabling through the power of the Spirit He has implanted within us? What goal in life is more sure of attainment than that to which the Almighty Himself has predestined us (Rom. 8:29) at the cost of His own Son's precious blood?

Our Father has made abundant provision for us to win the war against worldliness if only we will walk in the Spirit and allow Him to teach us to love what is truly lovely—not the world, but the One Who has overcome the world.

> O Sovereign of the universe,
> Who created all things good
> And one day will restore Your world's original goodness
> For the glory of Your name and the enjoyment of
>   Your people,
> Be pleased, I pray, to prosper this book's attempt
> To assist Your people in overcoming the evil world
> That has arisen through Your adversary's corrupt and
>   corrupting power.
>
> Haste the day, our Father,
> When shall appear that new heaven and new earth,
> Wherein dwelleth righteousness.
>
> And until then, our all-wise Shepherd,
> Direct our steps in the way of holiness,
> Creating and satisfying within us a hunger and thirst
>   for righteousness,
> That we may always love You
> And never love the world.
>
> In the name of Jesus Christ
> Your Son and our Savior
> I pray.
>
> Amen.